THE VEGAN COOKBOOK

THE VEGAN COOKBOOK

OVER 50 INSPIRATIONAL RECIPES THAT ARE FREE FROM ANIMAL PRODUCTS

CONSULTING AUTHOR

NICOLA GRAIMES

INTRODUCTION BY

AMANDA ROFE

LORENZ BOOKS

First published in 2000 by Lorenz Books

© Anness Publishing Limited 2000

Lorenz Books is an imprint of
Anness Publishing Inc.
27 West 20th Street
New York, NY 10011

ISBN 0 7548 0185 3

Publisher: Joanna Lorenz
Editor: Sarah Ainley
Designer: Penny Dawes
Photographers: Michelle Garrett, Dave King, William Lingwood,
Thomas Odulate, Sam Stowell
(Pictures on the following pages were supplied by Life File: pp6 top and pp19 bottom)
Recipes: Jacqueline Clarke, Carole Clements, Joanna Farrow, Silvana Franco,
Nicola Graimes, Kathy Mann, Lesley Mackley, Liz Trigg, Jennie Shapter,
Elizabeth Wolfe-Cohen
Dieticians: Clare Brain and Wendy Doyle

Printed and bound in Singapore

1 3 5 7 9 10 8 6 4 2

CONTENTS

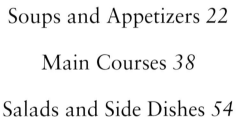

INTRODUCTION

An increasing number of people these days are making the transition toward an animal-free or vegan (pronounced "vee-gan") diet. If you have decided to become vegan, or if you are already vegan, this cookbook aims to provide the information you need to eat an exciting and healthy diet. In addition to using plant-based foods to create interesting and nutritional dishes, there is an increasing number of processed foods available that are suitable for vegans to use.

WHAT IS A VEGAN?

Veganism is defined as a way of living that excludes all forms of exploitation and cruelty to animals for food, clothing or any other purpose. A vegan is often referred to as a pure vegetarian because they have gone one step further than a lacto- or ovo-vegetarian, to exclude dairy products and eggs from their diet.

Most people begin their vegan lifestyle by making dietary changes. Meat, fish, poultry, eggs, animal milks, honey, and the derivatives of all of these, are replaced with plant-based products, such as fruits and vegetables, cereals, pulses, seeds and nuts, and soy products, such as soy milk and processed soy "mock" meats.

Other lifestyle changes are made by excluding other animal products— for example, by replacing leather, silk and wool products with man-made materials or cotton fabrics.

WHY BECOME A VEGAN?

The most common reason for becoming a vegan is to prevent, or at least to lessen, the exploitation and suffering of animals. Other reasons include health benefits, concern for the environment and spirituality.

ANIMAL SUFFERING

Animals are used for food, clothing, medical research and entertainment (circuses and zoos). Hundreds of millions of animals are slaughtered for meat every year, including cattle, sheep, pigs, ducks, fish, horses, game birds, hens and turkeys, geese, goats, rabbits, pheasant, deer, buffalo, whales, ostriches and kangaroos.

Above: The number of pesticides finding their way into dairy milk is on the increase.

HEALTH

The digestive and dental systems of human beings are "designed" for a plant-based diet. A vegan diet is low in fat and rich in fruits and vegetables. Meat, dairy products and eggs, on the other hand, contain no dietary fiber and are the principal sources of saturated fat and cholesterol in the diet.

An allergy to cow's milk is the most common food allergy in childhood, and scientific studies have implicated cow's milk consumption with heart disease and juvenile-onset diabetes. Meat, dairy products and eggs are known transmitters of food poisoning, such as salmonella, camylobacter, listeria and E coli. The artificial foodstuffs fed to farmed animals have an unknown effect on human beings.

Right: Animal milk dairy products are easily replaced with soy milk products.

ETHICS

More people around the world can be fed on a vegan diet than on one based on meat and dairy animal products, and a major shift towards veganism in industrialized countries would bring a radical fall in the price of plant foods.

The typical Western diet uses more than ten times the amount of grain we need in feeding animals alone. At present, 38 percent of the world's grain is fed to livestock, while millions of people in the Third World countries die every year from famine.

ECOLOGY

As the world's rainforests are destroyed to provide grazing land for beef cattle, intensive fishing is depleting fish stock, and wildlife habitats are threatened as trees are cut down to maximize farm land. The long-term realities of the animal-based diet are irreparable damage to the planet and the forced extinction of some of the world's rarest species.

SPIRITUALITY

Orthodox Buddhists and Hindus adhere to an animal-free diet that is based on the belief that all life forms are sacred, not just human life (as in Christianity). In addition to the ethics of veganism, they teach that a vegan diet is conducive to spiritual peace, and will promote feelings of humility and compassion, the qualities which are most admired in all religions.

VEGAN FOOD PRODUCTS

Shopping for animal-free products is easy once you know what to look for. As well as the more obvious vegan foods, such as fresh fruits and vegetables, there are a growing number of processed products suitable for vegans, from soy-based milks and cheeses to "mock" meats such as "turkey," "chicken" and "beef." Healthfood stores always stock vegan food, and the larger supermarkets are also increasing their stock of such products these days.

Food manufacturing and processing is a complex area, however, and it is important to remember that while some foods appear suitable for vegans, the ingredients listed on the packaging may include animal by-products, which are not easily identifiable. Check labels carefully before you buy. You will quickly learn to recognize the more common animal substances, but if in doubt, contact the manufacturer directly. Some supermarkets and vegan organizations provide lists of products that are entirely animal-free.

Above: Processed soy sausages have all the flavor of the real thing.

GLOSSARY OF COMMON ANIMAL BY-PRODUCTS

Albumen or **albumin** water-soluble proteins found in egg whites, milk and blood

Aspic savory jelly made from meat or fish

Beeswax★ waxy secretion from bees

Bone or **bonemeal** animal bones

Carmine or **carminic acid** red dye made from insects

Casein★ milk protein

Chitin rigid part of insects and crustacea

Cholecalciferol (D3) vitamin derived from lanolin or fish oil

Cod liver oil oil from the liver of fish

Drippings animal fat

Gelatin a thickening agent made by boiling animal skin and bone

Glycerine or **glycerol★** a clear liquid made from animal fat

Isinglass a pure form of gelatin, obtained from the air bladder of freshwater fish

Lactic acid acid produced by fermenting milk sugar

Lactose a sugar found in milk

Lanolin fat extracted from sheep's wool

Lecithin fatty substance derived from egg yolk

Propolis "glue" used by bees in hives

Rennet★ extract of calf stomach

Royal jelly food fed to bee larvae to develop the queen bee

Shellac insect secretion

Sodium 5'-inosinate prepared from fish waste

Stearic acid prepared from stearin

Stearin or **stearine★** main constituent of animal fat

Suet★ hard animal fat

Tallow white, solid animal fat

Whey residue from milk after the removal of casein and most of the fat

★ substance may be non-animal derived, contact manufacturer for details

AVOIDING ANIMAL PRODUCTS

Animal derivatives used in the manufacturing and processing of non-animal or dairy food products can be a cause of concern for vegans. The hidden ingredients can be identified by scientific analysis, but are rarely listed on the product's packaging because they have been introduced indirectly, during processing. The affected products are wide-ranging, and include staples, such as fresh fruit, vitamins and tap water. Vegan groups can recommend products and brands that are known to be animal-free, or you can contact manufacturers directly for details of processing procedures.

ADDITIVES

There are two main categories of food additives: those that prevent food from spoiling and those that enhance its flavor, texture or appearance. You may choose to avoid additives for health reasons, or because they are safety-tested on animals before they are allowed onto the market. There are thousands of additives used in processed foods worldwide, and they may or may not be animal-derived. Additives that are usually animal-derived include:

- cochineal
- edible bone phosphate
- sodium 5'-inosinate
- beeswax
- shellac
- calcium mesoinositol hexaphosphate
- lactose

Other additives may be either animal or non-animal in origin; there are few hard and fast rules in food processing, and the manufacturer is often the only one who will know for sure whether their product is suitable for vegans.

Right: Traces of either shellac or beeswax may be found on fresh fruit.
Far right: Wine, beer, poppadums, dried banana chips and chocolate may all contain unlabeled animal derivatives.

PRODUCTS WITH HIDDEN ANIMAL INGREDIENTS

Beer may be filtered using isinglass (a form of gelatin)

Beta-carotene used as an orange coloring and may be used with powdered gelatin

Chocolate semi-sweet chocolate may contain butterfat or may be contaminated with dairy-derived release agents, used to remove the chocolate from molds

Confectioners' sugar may contain egg white

Digestible capsules usually made from gelatin

Dried banana chips often glazed with honey

Flavorings may be animal-derived or may be held in an animal-derived carrier, such as lactose

Fresh fruit may be coated with shellac or beeswax

Poppadums often coated with shellac

Quorn the trade name for mycoprotein, a fermented micro-organism, which contains egg

Sugar production in the United Kingdom is free from animal derivatives, but production in other countries varies and may include the use of carbonized animal bone, used as a refining agent, or fish oil, used as an anti-foaming agent

Vegetable bouillon usually contains milk derivatives

Vegetable margarine usually contains milk or animal derivatives

Vitamin D more often D3 (cholecalciferol) rather than the vegan D2 (ergocalciferol). Vitamin D2 may be carried in gelatin powder

Water (tap) some water companies use carbonized animal bone to filter the water

Wine may be filtered using blood, bone, chitin, egg albumin, fish oil, gelatin, isinglass, marrow or milk

VEGAN NUTRITION

Veganism is suitable for people of all ages from birth onward, and there are nutrition guidelines that should form the basis of your diet. Research has shown that the human body can run extremely efficiently when fed exclusively on plant foods. Many healthcare professionals advocate a vegan diet because it can help reduce the risk of the illnesses commonly seen in people who eat a high-fat diet.

A HEALTHY DIET

The vegan diet is typically low in salt and fat and is free of cholesterol. It is rich in fibre (non-starch polysaccharides), carbohydrates and important vitamins.

Research has shown that people who follow a vegan diet have a lower risk of a number of chronic diseases, including heart disease, gallstones, diverticular disease, diabetes, kidney stones and cancer of the breast and colon. A vegan diet is known to be of value in reducing the inflammation of acute rheumatoid arthritis, correcting intestinal dysbiosis and controlling asthma.

A joint report by the World Cancer Research Fund and the American Institute for Cancer Research strongly recommends a plant-based diet. The report criticizes the meat and dairy industries for promoting their products with the message that they are important to a healthy diet, when cancer research proves the opposite.

The following food groups form the basis of a vegan diet. Eating a choice of foods from each of these groups on a daily basis will ensure a complete nutritional balance. A larger part of the diet should comprise cereals, fruits and vegetables, with smaller quantities of pulses, soy products, nuts and seeds, and minimal consumption of processed foods.

Above: Favorite cereal foods include bagels, bread, rice cakes, wheat and pasta.

CEREALS (GRAINS)
- barley, corn, millet, oats, rice, rye, semolina, wheat, "ancient grains" (amaranth, farro, kamut, quinoa)

FRUITS
- any fruit (fresh, dried, frozen, canned)

VEGETABLES
- any vegetable (fresh, dried, frozen, canned)

PULSES (LEGUMES)
- beans, peas and lentils (fresh, dried, frozen, sprouted, canned)

NUTS
- fresh nuts (ground, milled, whole)

SEEDS
- fresh seeds (ground, milled, sprouted, whole)

PROCESSED SOY
- mock meats, soy burgers, sausages or Textured Vegetable Protein (TVP)

Above: Processed soy products are easily substituted for meat and dairy foods.

VEGAN SOURCES OF NUTRIENTS

PROTEIN
- cereals, nuts, pulses, seeds, soy products

It is commonly believed that plant foods contain poor quality or incomplete protein. While some plants do contain less protein than animal products, all plants contain essential amino acids, the building blocks of protein. Many plant foods, such as soy, millet and quinoa, are excellent sources of protein.

The American Dietetic Association claims that plant sources of protein alone can provide adequate amounts of essential amino acids if a variety of plant foods are consumed and energy needs are met. Research suggests that complementary proteins do not need to be consumed at the same time to be of value, and that the consumption of various sources of amino acids over the course of the day should ensure adequate nitrogen retention and use for a healthy person.

CARBOHYDRATES
- cereals, fresh and dried fruit, pulses, potatoes

FATS
- nuts, seeds (and their oils), vegan margarine, avocados

Saturated fats, containing cholesterol, are found in animal fats and should be avoided on a vegan diet. Cholesterol is necessary for certain bodily functions, but the body produces enough of its own, and a dietary source is not required. Most plant foods do not contain saturated fats, with the exception of coconut and palm oil.

Hydrogenated fats, which are found in some processed products, are thought to act in much the same way as saturates, and these should be avoided where possible.

Two polyunsaturated fatty acids that are not made by the body are linoleic acid (omega-6 group) and alpha-linolenic acid (omega-3 group), known as essential fatty acids (EFAs).

Above: Protein is widely available in the vegan diet, so long as a wide range of cereals, nuts, pulses, seeds and soy milks are eaten.

Above: Carbohydrates, such as potatoes, oats and pasta, are easily included in the diet.

Good sources of EFAs include:
Linoleic acid oils made from corn, evening primrose, hempseed, safflower, soy, sunflower
Alpha-linolenic acid oils made from hempseed, linseed, pumpkin, canola, soy, walnut

VITAMINS
VITAMIN A
- (found in vegetables as beta-carotene) carrots, dark green leafy vegetables, mango, margarine, pumpkin, spinach, sweet potato, tomatoes

B GROUP VITAMINS
B1 (thiamine), B2 (riboflavin), Niacin, Biotin, Folic acid, Pantothenic acid, B6 (pyridoxine), B12 *(see section on B12 below)*
- dried fruit, green leafy vegetables, muesli, mushrooms, nuts, oats, potatoes, pulses, whole-grains, yeast extracts and fortified breakfast cereals contain many B vitamins, particularly B2 and B12

Vitamin B12
- fortified products such as some breakfast cereals, soy milks, yeast extracts, TVP

(Claims have been made that certain sea vegetables contain high amounts of B12, but these are usually analogues rather than true or active B12 that can be utilized by the body.)

Vitamin B12 is commonly sourced from meat and other animal products. It is made by bacteria living in animals (including humans) and the environment.

Problems that stem from a B12 deficiency usually include an inability to absorb B12 (lack of intrinsic factor). The B12 deficiency occurs in the general population, however, and is not particular to vegans. Only a tiny amount of B12 is required by the body, and stores may last for many years.

Left: Sunflower oil, almonds, avocados and vegan margarine are just some of the foods that will supply the body with the fatty acids it does not produce itself.

Left and far left: A wide selection of raw or lightly cooked fresh vegetables and fruits will ensure an adequate vitamin intake.

It is thought that the body can make its own B12, and recent research has shown that some plants absorb B12. However, additional research is required on these subjects before any firm conclusions can be drawn.

In the meantime, the recommended sources of B12 for vegans are regular supplements or fortified foods. The type of B12 *(cyanocobalamin)* used in supplements and fortified foods in the United Kingdom, Canada and the United States is better absorbed in old age than the B12 from meat, and people in their senior years are advised to take a supplement, whether or not they are vegans.

VITAMIN C
• berries, citrus fruits, currants, green vegetables, potatoes

VITAMIN D2
• action of sunlight on the skin (5–15 minutes per day), fortified products, such as vegan margarine and soy milk

Research shows that vitamin D is usually poorly supplied in all diets. Action of sunlight on the skin provides a lot of vitamin D. However, if you live in northern latitudes, have a dark skin tone or keep your skin covered when outdoors, you should ensure that you take a supplement or eat fortified foods. This is particularly important during autumn and winter, when there there is less sunlight. Vitamin D works with calcium to ensure strong bones.

VITAMIN E
• nuts, seeds, vegetable oils, wheatgerm, whole-grains

MINERALS
CALCIUM
• bok choy, broccoli, cereals, dark green leafy vegetables, figs, fortified soy milk and soy milk products, hard tap water, molasses, nuts, parsley, pulses, sea vegetables, seeds, tahini, tofu

Research shows that foods high in animal protein and salt (a typical meat-based diet) increase the loss of calcium from the body. However, calcium derived from curly kale or whole-wheat bread is absorbed by the body as well as or better than calcium from cow's milk. Ensure an adequate intake of calcium (and vitamin D2) for children and teenagers.

IODINE
• iodized salt, sea salt, sea vegetables (hijiki, kelp, nori, wakame)

IRON
• dried fruit, grains, green leafy vegetables, fortified breakfast cereals, molasses, nuts, parsley, pulses, sea vegetables, seeds, the use of cast iron pots and pans

Iron deficiency anemia is common in all diets. Although iron from plant foods is less well absorbed than iron from animal products, research has shown that iron intake is generally above average in the vegan diet. Consuming food or drink rich in vitamin C during mealtimes enhances iron absorption (vegan diets contain above average amounts of vitamin C).

ZINC
• cereals, pulses, nuts, parsley, wheat-germ

Above: Broccoli, tahini, sea vegetables and seeds will all supply calcium to the diet.

Above: Dried apricots, almonds, lentils and spinach make good sources of iron.

DAILY MENU IDEAS

A vegan diet is more accessible than many people imagine. You can make any dish suitable for a vegan simply by replacing the animal products. It isn't difficult and you don't need to be a dietitian or a qualified chef. Here are some popular menu ideas.

BREAKFAST

- hot oatmeal or fortified breakfast cereal with soy milk
- whole-wheat toast with vegan margarine or peanut butter
- soy sausages, fried mushrooms, grilled tomatoes, scrambled tofu, hash browns
- fresh fruit salad topped with soy yogurt
- baked beans on whole-wheat toast

Right and below: Simple breakfast ideas include seasonal fruit with soy yogurt and slices of toast with vegan margarine. Below right: Try a warming bowl of carrot and cilantro soup for lunch.

LUNCH AND DINNER

APPETIZERS

- watercress and "mock" ham salad
- sweet bell peppers stuffed with rice and mushrooms
- red bell pepper pâté and crackers
- garlic and herb bread
- carrot and cilantro soup
- vegetable crudités
- bean and vegetable salad with a vinaigrette dressing

Far left: Garlic and herb bread is easy to make, and is a favorite appetizer with vegans and non-vegans alike.
Left: A slice of fruit tart served with thick soy cream makes a delightful dessert.

MAIN COURSES

- spaghetti "bolognese" topped with vegan Parmesan cheese
- tagliatelle with garlic and tomato sauce
- vegetable and bean casserole
- vegetable biryani
- shepherd's pie made with beans and steamed vegetables
- veggie burger in a bun with a mixed salad
- mushroom risotto
- spicy tofu stir-fry

DESSERTS

- fresh fruit salad and soy cream
- rice pudding
- sherry trifle
- chocolate cake
- cheesecake
- fruit pie
- pancakes with maple syrup
- soy ice cream
- sorbet
- rhubarb crisp
- orange jelly
- chocolate or vanilla fudge

SNACKS

- fresh or dried fruit
- nuts and seeds
- raw vegetables with dips
- crackers, rolls or pita bread with a filling of your choice
- soy sausage rolls
- vegetable samosas
- spring rolls
- falafels
- spinach and potato turnovers
- muffins
- some chips and candies

DRINKS

Most mineral water, fruit juice, carbonated drinks, coffee and tea (served with or without soy or other plant-based milk) are suitable for vegans. Coffee substitutes, such as dandelion, barley or chicory, are also popular. Spirits are generally suitable for vegans, but beers and wines may not be, so remember to check with the manufacturer before you buy.

Left and below: For quick vegan snacks, serve sticks of raw carrot and celery with vegetable or soy dips, or TVP sausages.

REPLACING DAIRY PRODUCTS AND EGGS

It is surprisingly easy to replace dairy products and eggs, and there is an ever-growing variety of foods on the market to enable you to do so. You can make quiches using tofu, ice cream using soy milk, and jellies using agar-agar. You can even eat a full breakfast using soy sausages, scrambled tofu on toast, grilled tomatoes and "bacon" that looks and tastes exactly like bacon but is in fact made from soy. Very often, even non-vegans do not notice the difference.

SOY

WHAT IS SOY?
Soy is a bean related to clover, peas and alfalfa. It contains an excellent balance of amino acids, and is considered the equivalent in protein quality to meat, milk and eggs, which is one reason it has become so popular. Soy has made an enormous impact on the processed food market in the West in recent years and is now used in a variety of products.

WHERE DOES IT COME FROM?
For centuries, the soybean has been the basis of Asian cuisine, and is thought to have been cultivated in China for over 5,000 years. Many foods have been developed from soy, but the most popular are miso, soy milk, soy sauce, tempeh and tofu. More soybeans are grown in the United States than anywhere else in the world, although other producers include Brazil, Argentina and China. Soybeans and their derivatives are also used for a huge variety of non-food products such as paints, soaps, plastics, adhesives and fabrics.

HEALTH BENEFITS
Soybeans are unique among beans containing compounds called isoflavones. These molecules have structures similar to the estrogen produced in the body, hence the name plant- or phyto-estrogen. There are many classes of active non-nutrients with estrogenic activity, but interest has focused on the beneficial effects of a group of compounds belonging to the isoflavones. The two primary isoflavones in soybeans are daidzein and genistein. Research suggests soy may offer health benefits relating to heart disease, osteoporosis, menopause symptom relief and, possibly, cancer.

HIGH IN NUTRITION
Soybeans are high in protein, iron, calcium, zinc, B vitamins, vitamin E and fiber. Steamed tofu made with calcium sulfate contains over five times as much calcium as whole pasteurized cow's milk. Soy oil also contains the beneficial polyunsaturated fat. It is free from cholesterol and contains both linoleic and linolenic essential fatty acids.

MILK
Soy milk This is commonly used as a replacement for dairy milk. Various types of soy milk are available, including sweetened, unsweetened, concentrated, ready-to-drink and powdered. Flavored varieties of soy milk include banana, carob, chocolate and strawberry. Each product has a slightly different taste, and most people have their own preferred brand. Soy milk can be used in the same way as cow's milk—in tea, coffee, custard, rice pudding, creamed soup, white sauce or poured over breakfast cereal.
Other milks Rice, oat, pea and nut milks are available at healthfood stores. To make your own nut milk, add a handful of blanched almonds or cashews to 2 cups cold water and blend until smooth and creamy.

CREAMS AND DESSERTS
Soy cream This is usually purchased as a pouring cream, although whipped cream, cream cheeses and sour creams are also available.

Above: Dairy replacements made from soy include cream, milk, ice cream and yogurt.

Above: Soy cheeses are highly developed to resemble dairy cheeses in all but milk content. Clockwise from top, Double Gloucester-, Cheshire- and Cheddar-flavored vegan cheeses.

Above: Replacements are now available for use wherever eggs are needed. Clockwise from top left, cider vinegar, soy milk, mashed potatoes, seasoned tofu and baking soda.

Soy dessert A ready-to-use product that is similar in appearance and taste to custard. It is available in vanilla, chocolate, strawberry or carob flavors.
Soy ice cream There are many soy-based ice creams that look and taste exactly like their dairy-based counterparts. They are available in a variety of flavors.
Tofu Made from soy milk, tofu, or bean curd, has little flavor of its own but absorbs other flavors well and is highly versatile. Firm tofu is sold in a block, and can be seasoned and cubed for use in stews and stir-fries. A softer set tofu called "silken" tofu is a good substitute for milk or cream in soups, puddings and desserts. For a simple cream dessert, blend silken tofu with sugar or maple syrup, a little vegetable oil and a flavoring such as cocoa powder or vanilla extract.

YOGURT

Soy yogurt Plain, flavored and "live" and active cultures soy yogurts are available at healthfood stores and most supermarkets. Soy yogurts are made from soy milk, and are used in the same way as dairy yogurts.

CHEESE

Cheese Hard and soft vegan cheeses are now available, made from soy milk. Flavors include Cheddar, Cheshire, Gouda, Stilton or Edam. A Parmesan-style powdered cheese is also sold for use on pizzas and pastas.
Nutritional yeast flakes These "cheesy" tasting flakes are grown for the healthfood market (unlike brewer's yeast powder, which has a bitter taste, and is a by-product of the brewing industry). Use them to flavor sauces or sprinkle on top of hot savory dishes.

EGGS

Eggs that are not eaten on their own are used primarily to bind a dish or to lighten it, when air is whipped into the egg before it is mixed with other ingredients. Eggs are widely used in cooking, but there are many ways to replace them.
Binders Mashed potatoes or a thick stocks can be used to bind veggie burgers, nut roasts and other savory dishes. Soy milk or soy desserts can be used to bind sweet dishes or cakes.
Raising agents Baking powder, or a mix of cider vinegar and baking soda (which is ideal for chocolate cakes) are successful raising agents.
Whole egg replacers Seasoned firm tofu is commonly used as a straight replacement for whole eggs to make quiches, flans and eggless "scrambled eggs."

THE VEGAN KITCHEN

A varied use of ingredients is the secret to all good cooking. The vegan diet will include fresh vegetable produce and processed products, but you will also need a supply of staples to use as the base for interesting and substantial meals. Keep your kitchen cupboards stocked with basic ingredients so that soups, casseroles, breads and baked goods can be made whenever you want them.

KITCHEN CUPBOARD STAPLES

Agar-agar
Baking powder
Baking soda
Beans (dried or canned)
Brown rice syrup
Carob or cocoa powder
Fruit and vegetables (fresh, dried, canned or frozen)
Fruit spread or jam
Herbs and spices
Lentils (dried or canned)
Nuts
Oats and oatmeal

Peanut butter and tahini
Rice, couscous and bulghur wheat
Seitan
Soy sauce
Soy or other plant-based milk
Tempeh
Tofu (firm and silken)
Vegan margarine
Vegetable oil
Whole-wheat flour
Whole-wheat breads
Whole-wheat pasta
Yeast extract

Below: Useful staples such as baking powder, whole-wheat flour, oats, oatmeal, rice, couscous and cocoa will allow you to make impromptu baked goods, breads and pastries.

Above and below: Whole-wheat pastas (above) provide the base for any number of quick meals, while soy sauce, flavored vinegars and spices (below) make easy sauces and dressings to add variety.

GLOSSARY OF TYPICAL VEGAN FOODS

Agar-agar a colorless powder or flake derived from a sea vegetable and used to set jellies or molds

Arrowroot (kuzu) a fine white powder made from a tropical root and used to make a glaze or sauce

Basmati rice an aromatic rice made in India and Pakistan

Bean sprouts beans that have been soaked and left to sprout. Use in salads

Brown rice syrup a sweetener made from brown rice and grain

Bulghur wheat a nutty flavored cracked wheat used in salads

Carob powder a flour made from the seed of the carob or locust tree and used in place of cocoa

Couscous similar to bulghur wheat but lighter in color and quicker to cook

Creamed coconut a solid block of coconut extract used in both sweet and savory dishes

Garbanzo chickpeas

Hummus a dip made from puréed chickpeas

Miso made from fermented soybean paste; used in soups and stews

Natto fermented, cooked whole soybeans with a cheesy texture

Seitan made from flour gluten and used as a meat substitute

Soybean a round, creamy colored bean, similar in protein value to meat, and used to make soy milk, tofu, tempeh, yogurt and other processed soy products

Soy protein isolates the protein removed from defatted soy flakes—at 92% protein, the most highly refined soy protein available

Soy milk a milk substitute made from soybeans

Soy sauce a dark liquid made from fermented soybeans and used to flavor savory dishes

Tahini a paste made with sesame seeds and used with a similar texture to peanut butter

Tamari naturally fermented soy sauce

Tempeh an Indonesian food of fermented soybeans made into chunky tender slices

Tofu a firm white block or cream, made by curdling soy milk with a coagulant

TVP (TSP) stands for textured vegetable protein (textured soy protein). It is made from soybeans and is similar in texture and taste to ground beef or lamb

Wheat gluten *see seitan*

Whole-foods unrefined foods

Yeast extract a salty savory spread

Yuba the dried, thin skin that forms on the surface of soy milk as it cools

Above: Fresh fruits and vegetables add color, taste and texture to the vegan diet.

PREGNANCY AND CHILDREN

Many health professionals recognize a vegan diet to be nutritionally adequate for people of all ages, but at key life stages, such as pregnancy and during infancy, childhood and adolescence, the body is working at its hardest, and its nutritional needs should be given special priority. A sensible vegan diet can satisfy the body's needs to promote normal growth at these times. Plan the diet carefully to ensure that any deficiencies occurring in the body are adequately compensated for.

PRE-CONCEPTION

In addition to a varied whole-food vegan diet, with plenty of fruits and vegetables, you should ensure adequate intake of folic acid and B12, preferably through fortified foods or supplements.

PREGNANCY

For all women, vegan and non-vegan alike, the recommended intake of vitamins and minerals is higher during pregnancy. Increase your intake of folic acid, vitamin A (beta-carotene), B1 (thiamine), niacin, riboflavin, B12, D2, calcium, iron and zinc.

During pregnancy, the body's store of B12 is not readily available to the fetus, which builds up its supply from the mother's daily intake. If B12 intake is low during pregnancy, the fetus will not have adequate stores of the vitamin, and this may lead to a deficiency in the child at some point after birth.

Human milk is not a rich source of zinc, and breast-feeding infants draw on their own body reserves, laid down during the last three months in the womb. Adequate zinc intake should therefore be ensured.

The increase in calorie requirements during pregnancy is relatively small. There is little, if any, increase in calorie need during the first six months, but an extra 200 calories per day should be consumed during the third trimester. Pregnant teenagers will require more calories as their own bodies are still growing at this age.

Extra water is required for making additional blood for the mother, the baby and for the amniotic fluid. Drink at least four to six 7 fluid-ounce glasses per day of either water, fruit juice, soy milk or vegetable juice. Avoid large amounts of coffee and tea, as caffeine has been associated with various problems during pregnancy.

The basic advice for pregnant women on a vegan diet is to follow the nutritional guidelines established for all vegan adults, ensuring an increased quantity of varied vegan whole-foods. Many women (not just vegans) take a daily multi-vitamin and mineral supplement during pregnancy as extra insurance.

BREAST-FEEDING

The diet to follow when breast-feeding is similar to that recommended for pregnancy, although the intakes of calories, protein, calcium, magnesium, zinc, copper, selenium and vitamin B12 are slightly higher. Eating an increased quantity of varied vegan whole-foods is an ideal way to give yourself a nutritional boost. In particular, ensure an adequate regular vitamin B12 and D2 intake at this time.

BIRTH TO 6 MONTHS

From birth to 6 months all your baby's nutritional needs will be met by regular feedings of breast or bottled milk.

Breast milk provides a young baby with a natural and nutritionally balanced diet. Gradually your baby will move away from milk as the main source of nutrition, toward her first solid foods.

If you decide to use bottled milk, it is possible to purchase a vegan formula. Ask any vegan organization, healthfood store or pharmacy for details of vegan formulas currently available. Soy-based infant formulas can be used from birth onward. Standard soy milks used by adults should not be used as a straight replacement for breast or infant formula, as they do not contain the correct amount of nutrients for a baby.

FIRST FOODS

The classic "first food" is mashed banana. Other choices include cooked and blended apples, peaches, carrot or baby rice.

Begin feedings with breast or bottle milk and gradually increase the amount of solid food afterward. Solids should never be added to a bottle of milk. Do not add salt, sugar or spice to food. Move from solid food at one feeding per day to solids at two feedings and so on, following the baby's appetite and pace.

TIPS FOR MORNING SICKNESS

- eat several small meals a day
- avoid fried foods
- stay upright after eating
- eat dry crackers on waking or during the night
- try herbal teas, such as peppermint or chamomile

Remember that after four or five months of age, your baby may not receive enough vitamin B12 or D2 from breast milk if your body stores are depleted. Bottled infant formula and some fortified soy milks contain vitamin B12 and D2.

7 Months

In addition to breast or bottled milk, you can introduce blended oats, millet, rice or whole-wheat breakfast cereal to the baby's diet, and a variety of vegetables, such as cooked and mashed carrots, sweet potatoes and parsnips.

8-10 Months

Gradually adjust your baby's feedings to fit in with the family's meals. Provide foods that contain soft lumps, such as mashed potato, to get her used to using a spoon. Your baby will be ready for fresh fruits, such as pears, peaches, plums and melons. You can also try finger foods, such as toast or rusks. By now your baby may also be ready to take a drink from a cup. Suitable drinks, other than breast or bottled milk, include cooled boiled water or diluted fruit juices, such as apple or pear.

10-12 Months

Foods should be chopped, finely grated or blended. Your baby will be more inclined to hold a spoon, and may be moving toward eating on her own. A greater variety of vegetables should be offered at this point. Only introduce nut butters on the advice of your healthcare professional if you have a family history of nut allergies.

12+ Months

From 12 months of age your infant can share the same meals as the rest of the family, with additional snacks. Keep in mind the following key points:
Reduce fiber
- cook fruits with their skins on and peel them before serving
- use refined grain products, such as white rice and couscous

Above: Vegan infant formula milks are available at pharmacies and health stores.

Use energy-dense foods
- use fruit juices or concentrated fruit spreads
- use full fat and fortified soy milks or infant formula milk
- make thick oatmeal and add a little vegetable oil
- use nut butters, tahini and hummus
Use soy and canola oils
- use more soybean or canola (rapeseed) oil, and less sunflower, safflower and corn oils, to encourage brain and visual development
Boost vitamins and minerals
- use black molasses to increase iron and calcium intakes
- use tofu prepared with calcium sulfate (which contains more calcium than cow's milk)
- ensure access to sunshine and intake of vitamin D2 fortified foods
- ensure adequate vitamin B12 intake
- include vitamin C rich foods in meals to enhance iron absorption

Children and Teenagers

Vegetarianism among children is common, but many parents still feel veganism is a drastic step for a child or growing teenager. Conflict may arise when different foods have to be purchased and prepared. Older children and teenagers should make every effort to help with any extra shopping and meal preparation.

As a teenager facing hostility, answer any questions your family may have about your new diet calmly and sensibly, and avoid confrontation. Some parents will think it is a phase you are going through and may refuse to take your diet seriously. Others may think it will lead to ill health. You need to prove that your knowledge of nutrition is based on sound scientific fact, and that your meals are varied and healthy. Once these concerns have been dealt with, the transition toward an animal-free diet should be easier.

You should take time to plan how and when you are going to replace animal-derived products, rather than making a hurried overnight decision. This will ensure that you understand basic nutrition and menu ideas, allow your body to get used to new foods, and give family and friends time to warm to your new diet and lifestyle.

The diet recommendations for older children and teenagers are the same as for all vegans. A wide variety of whole-foods should be eaten daily, including fruits, vegetables, plenty of leafy greens, as well as whole-grain products, cereals, nuts, seeds and pulses.

Below: A varied vegan diet can satisfy nutritional demands at all ages.

Eating Out

Vegan travel guide books list cafés, restaurants, hotels and guesthouses that cater to vegans. The guides are available at tourist information centers and vegan organizations.

Visiting Family and Friends

If you are visiting relatives and friends it should be easy to organize the catering. Simply explain your requirements, send along some vegan recipes or offer to bring a dish to help out. If you are visiting for any length of time, provide your own staple vegan foods, such as soy milk, vegan margarine and vegan cheese.

Restaurants and Cafes

The number of places to eat that serve purely vegan food is increasing, but if you can't find a vegan restaurant, you may be able to find one that is strictly vegetarian. Vegetarian restaurants usually provide a good selection of vegan options on the menu. Indian restaurants are also a good choice, as they have a wide range of vegetable-based dishes.

When ordering food in a non-vegan restaurant, check the ingredients of the dish. It has been known for restaurants or cafés to have nothing suitable for vegans to eat, but this is becoming less common. If your local restaurant or café has no idea how to cater to vegans, offer to send them a vegan catering packet. Vegan organizations provide information packets especially for the catering industry.

Tips on Choosing Dishes

- pizza crusts may contain dairy derivatives
- soups may be made with meat, fish or chicken stock
- stock cubes/powder may contain dairy derivatives or animal fat
- vegetables may be cooked in the same oil as meat or fish
- cheese or margarine is typically never vegan (vegetarian cheese is not suitable for vegans)
- few desserts are vegan so choose fresh fruit salads instead
- ghee in Indian dishes may be clarified butter rather than vegetable
- unless a restaurant regularly caters to vegans, its staff is unlikely to know whether the wine or beer they serve is vegan

Plane Travel

Order a vegan meal for your flight when you make the plane reservation, and confirm it when you check in at the boarding desk a couple of hours before take off. Many airlines will provide a vegan meal, but you may have to call them up several times to ensure that you receive it.

Around the World

Manufacturing processes differ from country to country, and it is unlikely that you will find food products on vacation that contain exactly the same ingredients as the products you are used to at home. Take with you any products that you cannot live without.

Packed Lunches

Vegan food is not usually available in school and work cafeterias, or at highway rest stops. For this reason, a packed lunch is often needed.

- sandwiches, pita bread, bagels and rolls are tasty, cheap and easy to pack. Fill them with fresh salad vegetables, such as tomatoes, lettuce, scallions, cucumbers and coleslaw, as well as soy cheese, vegetable pâté, "mock" meat slices or hummus
- pack small cartons or bottles of fruit juice, soy milk and mineral water if you are on the move and won't have access to drinks
- vegan pre-packaged pastas and cup-of-soups are available at healthfood stores to provide a quick hot snack during the winter months
- small containers of soy yogurt are useful to pack for children's lunches
- pack fresh fruits, such as bananas and apples, for easy "desserts"
- sealed packages of dried fruit, nuts, cookies, crackers and rice cakes provide healthy snacks

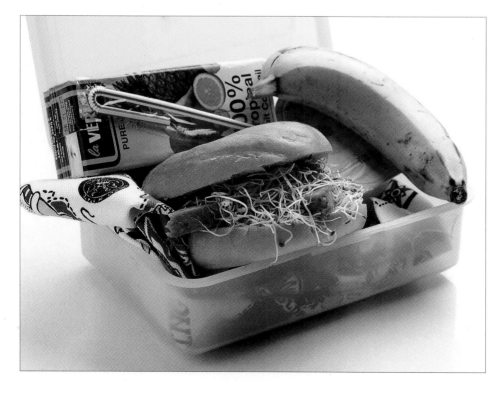

Left: A child's packed school lunch needs to be tasty and interesting. A bagel filled with salad and "mock" meat, a soy yogurt, a juice drink and fresh fruit is a popular and nutritious vegan lunch menu.

ENTERTAINING FAMILY AND FRIENDS

Once you feel confident cooking vegan meals, you will begin entertaining friends and family. Many non-vegans are surprised and impressed by the emphasis vegans place on fresh vegetable produce, flavor and creative cooking. You may even be asked to provide recipes, so be prepared.

ADAPTING DISHES

Any recipe can be adapted for a vegan diet, and there are no limits to the creations that can be produced. Meat is easily replaced with the soybean substitute for ground meat, TVP, and cow's milk with soy milk. Serve soy cheese and pickles with thick, crusty bread, or mix up your own garlicky mayonnaise with concentrated soy milk, garlic, oil, lemon juice and seasoning. Even trifles can be made by setting fruit juice with agar-agar, topping it with soy-milk custard, and finishing with a whipped soy cream. It is simply a matter of choosing the appropriate non-animal alternatives.

TIPS ON CHOOSING DISHES

When deciding on your dinner party menu, it is a good idea to choose familiar dishes, at least to begin with. If your friends and family have always eaten traditional homemade fare, they will be particularly suspicious of an exotic dish they have never heard of before. However, don't be afraid to be adventurous for more feisty guests.

When catering to your vegan child and her non-vegan friends, avoid introducing what non-vegans may think of as strange new foods—if the food is rejected by the friends, your child will be made to feel different and awkward. Children can be undiplomatic when it comes to food they don't like.

For children who are not used to whole-foods, be sure to use white bread or white rice. Soy sausage rolls made with puff pastry (instead of homemade whole-wheat pastry) will be accepted without question. Some companies produce ready-to-eat desserts set with carrageenan (a red algae) instead of gelatin, and these are popular with children, as are strawberry soy ice cream and chocolate soy milk shakes.

MAKE AN EFFORT

Some non-vegan people may make judgments on your vegan diet and lifestyle before they have experienced it themselves, and it is worth making an effort with the food you provide. There is no need to apologize for the food, as well-prepared vegan cuisine is always popular, and even cynical guests will be unable to find anything critical to say about it. Indeed, many people will not be able to tell whether the food they have eaten is vegan or not.

SUGGESTED MENUS

MENU 1
Cream of asparagus soup
Garlic and herb focaccia
Stir-fried tofu and vegetables with
   wild rice
Chocolate cheesecake and soy cream
Cheese and cookies
Coffee with soy cream

Above: Cheesecakes are a perennial favorite.

MENU 2
Mushroom pâté with ciabatta
Almond paella
Selection of steamed vegetables
Vanilla cream cake
Chocolate mints
Coffee with soy cream

Above: Pasta served with a vegan fresh basil pesto makes an ideal supper dish.

SOUPS AND APPETIZERS

For anyone inspired by unusual ingredients and flavor-combinations,

this selection of vegan soups offers endless possibilities. Each recipe has

been lovingly created to get the most from its ingredients, and the

result is a range of fresh-tasting soups with a wonderful depth of

flavor. For unbeatable appetizers, serve Mediterranean-style olives

marinated in fresh herbs, spicy Greek dolmades or roasted potato wedges

with a hot chili dip. Or try sizzling stir-fries for a taste of Asia.

Italian Pea and Basil Soup

Plenty of crusty country bread is a must with this vividly colored, fresh-tasting soup.

INGREDIENTS

Serves 4
5 tablespoons olive oil
2 large onions, chopped
1 celery stalk, chopped
1 carrot, chopped
1 garlic clove, finely chopped
3½ cups frozen peas
3¾ cups vegetable stock
1 cup fresh basil leaves, roughly torn, plus extra to garnish
salt and freshly ground black pepper
vegan parmesan cheese, to serve (optional)

1 Heat the oil in a large saucepan and add the onions, celery and carrot and garlic. Cover the pan and cook over low heat for 45 minutes or until the vegetables are soft. Stir occasionally to prevent the vegetables from sticking to the bottom of the pan.

--- NUTRITION NOTES ---

Per portion:

Calories	208
Protein	6.4g
Fat	14.8g
Saturated Fat	2.2g
Carbohydrate	12.9g
Fiber	5.9g
Iron	2.1mg
Calcium	64.2mg

2 Add the peas and stock to the pan and bring to a boil. Reduce the heat, add the basil and seasoning, then simmer for 10 minutes.

3 Process the soup in a food processor, or using a blender, for a few minutes, until the texture is smooth. Transfer to bowls, sprinkle with vegan parmesan, if using, and garnish with torn basil leaves.

Spiced Red Lentil and Coconut Soup

Hot, spicy and richly flavored, this substantial soup is almost a meal in itself. If you are really hungry, serve with warmed naan.

INGREDIENTS

Serves 4
2 tablespoons sunflower oil
2 red onions, finely chopped
1 bird's eye chile, seeded and finely sliced
2 garlic cloves, chopped
1-inch piece fresh lemongrass, outer layers removed and inside finely sliced
1 cup red lentils, rinsed
1 teaspoon ground coriander
1 teaspoon paprika
1⅔ cups coconut milk
juice of 1 lime
3 scallions, chopped
scant 1 cup cilantro, finely chopped
salt and freshly ground black pepper

1 Heat the oil in a large, deep frying pan and add the onions, chile, garlic and lemongrass. Cook for 5 minutes or until the onions have softened, stirring occasionally.

--- NUTRITION NOTES ---

Per portion:

Calories	244
Protein	12.8g
Fat	6.6g
Saturated Fat	0.9g
Carbohydrate	35.7g
Fiber	2.9g
Iron	4.2mg
Calcium	69.7mg

2 Add the lentils and spices. Pour in the coconut milk and 3¾ cups water, and stir. Bring to a boil, stir, then reduce the heat and simmer for 40–45 minutes or until the lentils are soft and mushy.

3 Pour in the lime juice and add the scallions and cilantro, reserving a little of each for the garnish. Season, then ladle into bowls. Garnish with the reserved scallions and cilantro.

Japanese-style Noodle Soup

This invigorating soup is flavored with just a hint of chile. It is best served as a light lunch or as a first course. According to Japanese etiquette, slurping while eating soup is a sign of appreciation.

INGREDIENTS

Serves 4
3 tablespoons mugi miso
  (soybean paste)
2 scant cups udon noodles or
  soba noodles
2 tablespoons sake or dry sherry
1 tablespoon rice or wine vinegar
3 tablespoons Japanese soy sauce
4 ounces asparagus tips or snowpeas,
  thinly sliced diagonally
scant 1 cup shiitake mushrooms, stems
  removed and thinly sliced
1 carrot, sliced into julienne strips
3 scallions, thinly sliced diagonally
1 teaspoon dried chile flakes, to serve
salt and freshly ground black pepper

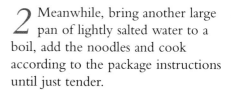

1 Bring 4 cups water to a boil in a saucepan. Pour ⅔ cup of the boiling water over the miso and stir until dissolved, then set aside.

NUTRITION NOTES	
Per portion:	
Calories	217
Protein	7.2g
Fat	3.4g
Saturated Fat	0.0g
Carbohydrate	39.8g
Fiber	2.5g
Iron	1.3mg
Calcium	28.5mg

2 Meanwhile, bring another large pan of lightly salted water to a boil, add the noodles and cook according to the package instructions until just tender.

3 Drain the noodles in a colander. Rinse under cold running water, then drain again.

4 Add the sake or sherry, rice or wine vinegar and soy sauce to the pan of boiling water. Boil gently for 3 minutes or until the alcohol has evaporated, then reduce the heat and stir in the miso mixture. Add the asparagus or snowpeas, mushrooms, carrot and scallions, and simmer for about 2 minutes until the vegetables are just tender. Season to taste.

5 Divide the noodles among four warm bowls and pour the soup over the top. Serve immediately, sprinkled with the chile flakes.

Roasted Root Vegetable Soup

Roasting the vegetables gives this winter soup a wonderful depth of flavor. You can use other vegetables, if desired, depending on what's in season.

INGREDIENTS

Serves 6
¼ cup olive oil
1 small butternut squash, peeled, seeded and cubed
2 carrots, cut into thick rounds
1 large parsnip, cubed
1 small rutabaga, cubed
2 leeks, thickly sliced
1 onion, quartered
3 bay leaves
4 fresh thyme sprigs, plus extra to garnish
3 fresh rosemary sprigs
5 cups vegetable stock
salt and freshly ground black pepper
thick soy yogurt, to serve

1 Preheat the oven to 400°F. Put the olive oil into a large bowl. Add the prepared vegetables and toss until coated in the oil.

2 Place the vegetables in a single layer on two baking sheets. Tuck the bay leaves, thyme and rosemary into the vegetables.

3 Roast for 50 minutes, until tender, turning the vegetables occasionally to make sure they brown evenly all over. Remove from the oven, discard the herbs and transfer the vegetables to a large saucepan.

4 Pour the stock into the pan and bring to a boil. Reduce the heat, season to taste, then simmer for 10 minutes. Transfer the soup to a food processor or blender (or use a hand blender) and process for a few minutes until thick and smooth.

5 Return the soup to the pan to heat through. Season and serve with a spoonful of soy yogurt. Garnish each serving with a sprig of thyme.

----- COOK'S TIP -----

Dried herbs can be used in place of fresh; use ½ teaspoon of each type and sprinkle on the vegetables in Step 2.

----- NUTRITION NOTES -----

Per portion:

Calories	102
Protein	1.6g
Fat	6.6g
Saturated Fat	0.9g
Carbohydrate	9.7g
Fiber	3.2g
Iron	0.9mg
Calcium	57.8mg

Spicy Peanut Soup

A thick and warming vegetable soup, richly flavored with chili powder and peanuts.

INGREDIENTS

Serves 6

2 tablespoons oil
1 large onion, finely chopped
2 garlic cloves, crushed
1 teaspoon mild chili powder
2 red bell peppers, seeded and finely chopped
8 ounces carrots, finely chopped
8 ounces potatoes, peeled and cubed
3 celery stalks, sliced
3¾ cups vegetable stock
6 tablespoons crunchy peanut butter
⅔ cup corn
salt and freshly ground black pepper
roughly chopped unsalted roasted peanuts, to garnish

1 Heat the oil in a large pan and cook the onion and garlic for about 3 minutes. Add the chili powder and cook for another minute.

2 Add the peppers, carrots, potatoes and celery to the pan. Stir well, then cook for another 4 minutes, stirring occasionally.

3 Stir in the stock, peanut butter and corn until combined.

4 Season well. Bring to a boil, cover and simmer for 20 minutes or until all the vegetables are tender. Adjust the seasoning before serving, and sprinkle with the chopped roasted peanuts, to garnish.

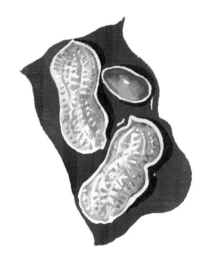

NUTRITION NOTES	
Per portion:	
Calories	209
Protein	6.6g
Fat	12.8g
Saturated Fat	2.3g
Carbohydrate	17.8g
Fiber	3.8g
Iron	1.1mg
Calcium	37.1mg

Fresh Tomato and Bean Soup

A rich chunky tomato soup, with beans and cilantro. Serve with olive ciabatta.

INGREDIENTS

Serves 4

2 pounds ripe plum tomatoes
2 tablespoons olive oil
10 ounces onions, roughly chopped
2 garlic cloves, crushed
3¾ cups vegetable stock
2 tablespoons sun-dried tomato paste
2 teaspoons paprika
1 tablespoon cornstarch
15-ounce can cannellini beans, rinsed
    and drained
2 tablespoons chopped cilantro
salt and freshly ground black pepper
olive ciabatta, to serve

1 First, peel the tomatoes. Using a sharp knife, make a small cross in each one and place in a bowl. Pour in boiling water to cover and let stand for 30–60 seconds.

2 Drain the tomatoes and peel off the skins. Quarter them and then cut each piece in half again.

3 Heat the oil in a large saucepan and cook the onions and garlic for 3 minutes, until soft.

4 Add the tomatoes to the onions, with the stock, sun-dried tomato paste and paprika. Season with a little salt and pepper. Bring to a boil and simmer for 10 minutes.

5 Mix the cornstarch to a paste with 2 tablespoons water. Stir the beans into the soup with the cornstarch paste. Cook for another 5 minutes. Adjust the seasoning and stir in the chopped cilantro just before serving.

NUTRITION NOTES	
Per portion:	
Calories	263
Protein	9.6g
Fat	10.7g
Saturated Fat	1.6g
Carbohydrate	34.5g
Fiber	9.6g
Iron	4.2mg
Calcium	105mg

Salsa Verde

There are many versions of this classic green salsa. Serve this one with corn tortilla chips or as a topping for bruschetta.

INGREDIENTS

Serves 4
2–4 green chiles
8 scallions
2 garlic cloves
2 ounces salted capers
grated zest and juice of 1 lime
juice of 1 lemon
6 tablespoons olive oil
about 1 tablespoon green
   Tabasco sauce, to taste
1 fresh tarragon sprig
bunch of fresh parsley
freshly ground black pepper

1 Halve the chiles and remove their seeds. Trim the scallions and halve the garlic, then place in a food processor. Pulse briefly until all the ingredients are roughly chopped.

2 Use your fingertips to rub any excess salt off the capers but do not rinse them (see Variation). Add the capers, tarragon and parsley to the food processor and pulse again until they are finely chopped.

3 Transfer the mixture to a small bowl. Stir in the lime zest and juice, lemon juice and olive oil. Stir the mixture lightly so the citrus juice and oil do not emulsify.

4 Add green Tabasco and black pepper to taste. Chill until ready to serve, but do not prepare more than 8 hours in advance.

--- VARIATION ---

If you can find only capers pickled in vinegar, they can be used for this salsa but must be rinsed well in cold water first.

--- NUTRITION NOTES ---

Per portion:

Calories	161
Protein	1.0g
Fat	16.7g
Saturated Fat	2.33g
Carbohydrate	1.9g
Fiber	0.9g
Iron	1.0mg
Calcium	29mg

Cannellini Bean Dip

Spread this soft bean dip or pâté on wheat crackers or toasted pitas. Alternatively, it can be served with wedges of tomato and a fresh green salad.

INGREDIENTS

Serves 4
14-ounce can cannellini beans
grated zest and juice of 1 lemon
2 tablespoons olive oil
1 garlic clove, finely chopped
2 tablespoons chopped fresh parsley
red Tabasco sauce, to taste
cayenne pepper
salt and freshly ground black pepper

1 Drain the cannellini beans in a sieve and rinse them well under cold running water. Transfer to a shallow bowl.

2 Use a potato masher to roughly purée the beans, then stir in the lemon zest and juice and olive oil.

3 Stir in the garlic and parsley. Add Tabasco sauce and salt and pepper.

4 Spoon the dip into a bowl and dust lightly with cayenne pepper. Chill until ready to serve.

--- NUTRITION NOTES ---

Per portion:

Calories	121
Protein	5.2g
Fat	6.3g
Saturated Fat	0.77g
Carbohydrate	11.8g
Fiber	3.6g
Iron	1.6mg
Calcium	47mg

--- VARIATION ---

Other beans can be used for this dish, if preferred, for example, lima beans or kidney beans.

Olives with Moroccan Marinades

INGREDIENTS

Serves 6
1⅓ cups green or tan olives (unpitted)
   for each marinade

For the Moroccan marinade
3 tablespoons chopped cilantro
3 tablespoons chopped fresh
   flat-leaf parsley
1 garlic clove, finely chopped
good pinch of cayenne pepper
good pinch of ground cumin
2–3 tablespoons olive oil
2–3 tablespoons lemon juice

For the spicy herb marinade
¼ cup chopped cilantro
¼ cup chopped fresh
   flat-leaf parsley
1 garlic clove, finely chopped
1 teaspoon grated fresh ginger root
1 red chile, seeded and finely sliced
¼ preserved lemon, cut into
   thin strips (optional)

1 Crack the olives, hard enough to break the flesh but without cracking the pit. Place in a bowl of cold water and let sit overnight to remove the excess brine. Drain thoroughly and place in a bowl.

2 Blend the ingredients for the Moroccan marinade and pour over half the olives, adding more olive oil and lemon juice to cover, if necessary. Place in a jar.

3 Mix the ingredients for the spicy herb marinade. Add the remaining olives and place in a jar. Store both jars in the refrigerator for at least 1 week before use, shaking them occasionally.

NUTRITION NOTES	
Per portion (average of 2 marinades):	
Calories	75
Protein	1.2g
Fat	7.3g
Saturated Fat	0.98g
Carbohydrate	1.2g
Fiber	1.5g
Iron	1.8mg
Calcium	58mg

Byesar

The Arab dish byesar is similar to Middle Eastern hummus, but uses fava beans instead of chickpeas. In Morocco, it is eaten by dipping bread into ground spices and then scooping up the purée.

INGREDIENTS

Serves 6
4 ounces dried fava beans, soaked
2 garlic cloves, peeled
1 teaspoon cumin seeds
about ¼ cup olive oil
salt
fresh mint sprigs, to garnish
extra cumin, cayenne pepper and fresh
   crusty bread, to serve

1 Put the dried fava beans in a casserole or pan with the whole garlic cloves and cumin seeds and add enough water just to cover. Bring to a boil, then reduce the heat and simmer until the beans are tender. Drain, cool and then slip off the outer skin of each bean.

2 Purée the beans in a blender or food processor, adding sufficient olive oil and water to give a smooth soft dip. Season to taste with plenty of salt. Garnish with sprigs of mint and serve with extra cumin seeds, cayenne pepper and bread.

NUTRITION NOTES	
Per portion:	
Calories	177
Protein	8.0g
Fat	11.8g
Saturated Fat	1.54g
Carbohydrate	10.2g
Fiber	8.0g
Iron	2.7mg
Calcium	44mg

Spiced Dolmades

These dolmades contain sumac, a spice with a sharp lemon flavor. It is available from specialty food stores.

INGREDIENTS

Makes 20
20 vacuum-packed grape leaves
   in brine
½ cup long-grain rice
3 tablespoons olive oil
1 small onion, finely chopped
⅔ cup pine nuts
¼ cup raisins
2 tablespoons chopped fresh mint
½ teaspoon ground cinnamon
½ teaspoon ground allspice
2 teaspoons ground sumac
2 teaspoons lemon juice
2 tablespoons tomato paste
salt and freshly ground black pepper
fresh mint sprigs, to garnish
garlicky soy yogurt and pita bread,
   to serve (optional)

1 Rinse the grape leaves well under cold running water, then drain. Bring a saucepan of lightly salted water to a boil. Add the rice, lower the heat, cover and simmer for 10–12 minutes, until almost cooked. Drain.

2 Heat 2 tablespoons of the olive oil in a frying pan, add the onion and cook until soft. Stir in the pine nuts and cook until lightly browned, then add the raisins, mint, cinnamon, allspice and sumac, with salt and pepper to taste. Stir in the rice and mix well. Let cool.

3 Line a saucepan with any damaged grape leaves. Trim the stems from the remaining leaves and lay them flat. Place a little filling on each. Fold the sides over and roll up each leaf neatly. Place the dolmades side by side in the leaf-lined pan, so that they fit tightly.

4 Mix 1¼ cups water with the lemon juice and tomato paste in a bowl. Add the remaining olive oil. Pour over the dolmades and place a heatproof plate on top to keep them in place.

5 Cover the pan and simmer the dolmades for 1 hour, until the liquid has been absorbed and the leave are tender. Transfer to a platter, garnish with fresh mint and serve.

───── VARIATION ─────

Fresh grape leaves may be used but must be blanched in boiling water first to make them pliable.

───── NUTRITION NOTES ─────

Per dolmade:

Calories	59
Protein	0.8g
Fat	3.4g
Saturated Fat	0.3g
Carbohydrate	6.5g
Fiber	0.2g
Iron	0.4mg
Calcium	7.5mg

Spicy Potato Wedges with Chili Dip

For an easy appetizer with superb flavor, try these roasted potato wedges. The spiced crust makes them irresistible, especially when served with a chili dip.

INGREDIENTS

Serves 2
2 baking potatoes, about 8 ounces each
2 tablespoons olive oil
2 garlic cloves, crushed
1 teaspoon ground allspice
1 teaspoon ground coriander
1 tablespoon paprika
salt and freshly ground black pepper

For the dip
1 tablespoon olive oil
1 small onion, finely chopped
1 garlic clove, crushed
7-ounce can chopped tomatoes
1 fresh red chile, seeded and
　finely chopped
1 tablespoon balsamic vinegar
1 tablespoon chopped cilantro,
　plus extra sprigs to garnish

1 Preheat the oven to 400°F. Cut the potatoes in half, then into eight wedges.

2 Place the wedges in a saucepan of cold water. Bring to a boil, then lower the heat and simmer gently for 10 minutes or until the potatoes have softened slightly. Drain well and pat dry on paper towels.

3 Mix the oil, garlic, allspice, coriander and paprika in a roasting pan. Add salt and pepper to taste. Add the potatoes to the pan and shake to coat them thoroughly. Roast for 20 minutes, turning the potato wedges occasionally or until they are browned, crisp and fully cooked.

4 Meanwhile, make the chili dip. Heat the oil in a saucepan, add the onion and garlic and cook for 5–10 minutes, until soft. Add the tomatoes, with their juice. Stir in the chile and vinegar. Cook gently for 10 minutes, until the mixture has reduced and thickened, then check the seasoning. Stir in the cilantro and serve hot, with potato wedges. Garnish with cilantro.

COOK'S TIP

These spicy potato wedges are equally delicious served with hummus or a homemade dairy-free mayonnaise.

NUTRITION NOTES

Per portion:

Calories	344
Protein	6.1g
Fat	17.1g
Saturated Fat	2.1g
Carbohydrate	44.1g
Fiber	4.0g
Iron	1.5mg
Calcium	31mg

Spiced Vegetables with Coconut

This spicy and substantial dish could be served as an appetizer for four, or as a vegan main course for two. Eat it with hunks of bread for mopping up the delicious coconut milk.

INGREDIENTS

Serves 4
1 red chile
2 large carrots
6 celery stalks
1 bulb fennel
2 tablespoons grapeseed oil
1-inch piece ginger root, peeled and grated
1 clove garlic, crushed
3 scallions, sliced
14-ounce can thin coconut milk
1 tablespoon cilantro, chopped
salt and freshly ground black pepper
cilantro sprigs, to garnish

1 Halve, de-seed and finely chop the chile. If necessary, wear rubber gloves to protect your hands.

2 Slice the carrots and celery stalks on the diagonal, using a sharp knife or cleaver.

— NUTRITION NOTES —	
Per portion:	
Calories	100
Protein	1.5g
Fat	6.2g
Saturated Fat	0.8g
Carbohydrate	10.3g
Fiber	2.6g
Iron	0,8mg
Calcium	78mg

3 Trim the fennel head and slice roughly, using a sharp knife.

4 Heat the wok, then add the oil. When the oil is hot, add the ginger and garlic, chile, carrots, celery, fennel and scallions and stir-fry for 2 minutes.

5 Gradually stir in the coconut milk and bring to a boil.

6 Stir in the cilantro and salt and pepper, garnish with cilantro sprigs and serve.

Bok Choy and Mushroom Stir-fry

Try to buy all the varieties of mushroom for this dish; the wild oyster and shiitake mushrooms have particularly distinctive, delicate flavors.

INGREDIENTS

Serves 4
4 dried black Chinese mushrooms
1 pound bok choy
2 ounces oyster mushrooms
2 ounces shiitake mushrooms
1 tablespoon vegetable oil
1 clove garlic, crushed
2 tablespoons oyster sauce

1 Soak the black Chinese mushrooms in ⅔ cup boiling water for 15 minutes to soften.

2 Tear the bok choy into bite-size pieces with your fingers.

3 Halve any large oyster or shiitake mushrooms, using a sharp knife.

4 Strain the Chinese mushrooms. Heat the wok, then add the oil. When the oil is hot, stir-fry the garlic until softened but not colored.

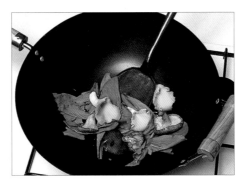

5 Add the bok choy and stir-fry for 1 minute. Mix in all the mushrooms and stir-fry for 1 minute.

6 Add the oyster sauce, toss well to coat the bok choy and mushrooms, and serve immediately.

NUTRITION NOTES	
Per portion:	
Calories	64
Protein	3.1g
Fat	3.1g
Saturated Fat	0.35g
Carbohydrate	6.6g
Fiber	0.2g
Iron	2.9mg
Calcium	66mg

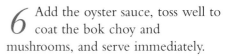

MAIN COURSES

Vegans really know how to make fabulous-tasting dishes from the

most basic ingredients. Grains and pulses, such as rice, wheat,

noodles, beans and pasta, are nutritious and easy to handle, and they

form the backdrop for the wealth of color and flavor provided by

vegetables, herbs and spices. There are stir-fries, stews, pastas and pies

here: the base ingredients are staples, while fresh produce can be

adapted to whatever is available.

Spiced Tofu Stir-fry

Any cooked vegetable could be added to this tasty stir-fry.

INGREDIENTS

Serves 4

2 teaspoons ground cumin
1 tablespoon paprika
1 teaspoon ground ginger
1 tablespoon sugar
10 ounces tofu
4 tablespoons olive oil
2 garlic cloves, crushed
1 bunch scallions, sliced
1 red bell pepper, seeded and sliced
1 yellow bell pepper, seeded and sliced
generous 3 cups brown-cap
  mushrooms, halved or quartered,
  if necessary
1 large zucchini, sliced
4 ounces green beans, halved
scant ⅔ cup pine nuts
1 tablespoon lime juice
1 tablespoon maple syrup
good pinch of cayenne pepper
salt and freshly ground black pepper

1 In a bowl, combine the cumin, paprika, ginger, cayenne and sugar with plenty of seasoning. Cut the tofu into cubes and coat the cubes in the spice mixture.

2 Heat half the oil in a wok or large frying pan. Cook the tofu over high heat for 3–4 minutes, turning occasionally (be careful not to break up the tofu too much). Remove with a slotted spoon and set aside. Wipe out the pan with paper towels.

3 Add the remaining oil to the wok or pan and cook the garlic and scallions for 3 minutes. Add the remaining vegetables and cook over medium heat for 6 minutes or until they are beginning to soften and turn golden. Season well.

4 Return the tofu to the wok or pan and add the pine nuts, lime juice and maple syrup. Heat through and serve immediately.

NUTRITION NOTES	
Per portion:	
Calories	309
Protein	10.8g
Fat	23.3g
Saturated Fat	3.3g
Carbohydrate	14.8g
Fiber	3.5g
Iron	3.3mg
Calcium	393mg

Teriyaki Soba Noodles with Tofu and Asparagus

You can, of course, buy ready-made teriyaki sauce but it is easy to prepare at home using ingredients that are now readily available at supermarkets and specialty stores. Japanese soba noodles are made from buckwheat flour, which gives them a unique texture and color.

INGREDIENTS

Serves 4

12 ounces soba noodles
2 tablespoons toasted sesame oil
½ bunch asparagus tips
2 tablespoons peanut or
   vegetable oil
8 ounces tofu
2 scallions, cut into thin strips
1 carrot, cut into matchsticks
½ teaspoon chile flakes
1 tablespoon sesame seeds
salt and freshly ground black pepper

For the teriyaki sauce
¼ cup dark soy sauce
¼ cup Japanese sake or
   dry sherry
¼ cup mirin
1 teaspoon sugar

1 Cook the noodles according to the instructions on the package, then drain and rinse well under cold running water. Set aside.

2 Heat the sesame oil in a frying pan or on a baking sheet until very hot. Turn down the heat to medium, then cook the asparagus for 8–10 minutes, turning frequently, until tender and browned. Set aside.

3 Meanwhile, heat the peanut or vegetable oil in a wok or large frying pan until very hot. Add the tofu and fry for 8–10 minutes, until golden, turning it occasionally to crisp all sides. Carefully remove from the wok or pan and let drain on paper towels. Cut the tofu into ½-inch slices with a sharp knife.

4 To prepare the teriyaki sauce, combine the soy sauce, sake or dry sherry, mirin and sugar, then heat the mixture in the wok or frying pan.

5 Toss in the noodles and stir to coat them in the sauce. Heat through for 1–2 minutes, then spoon into warmed individual serving bowls with the tofu and asparagus. Sprinkle on the scallions, carrot, chile flakes and sesame seeds. Serve immediately.

--- VARIATION ---

Use rice or cellophane (mung bean) noodles instead of soba noodles, if desired.

--- NUTRITION NOTES ---

Per portion:

Calories	490
Protein	10.5g
Fat	13.8g
Saturated Fat	1.7g
Carbohydrate	73g
Fiber	1.3g
Iron	2.6mg
Calcium	319mg

Pilaf with Saffron and Pickled Walnuts

Pickled walnuts have a warm, tangy flavor that is perfect in rice and bulghur wheat dishes. This Eastern Mediterranean pilaf is interesting enough to serve on its own or with a selection of grilled vegetables.

INGREDIENTS

Serves 4
1 teaspoon saffron threads
⅔ cup pine nuts
3 tablespoons olive oil
1 large onion, chopped
3 garlic cloves, crushed
¼ teaspoon ground allspice
1½-inch piece fresh ginger root, grated
generous 1 cup long-grain rice
1¼ cups vegetable stock
½ cup pickled walnuts, drained and roughly chopped
¼ cup raisins
3 tablespoons roughly chopped fresh parsley or cilantro, plus extra leaves to garnish
salt and freshly ground black pepper
plain soy yogurt, to serve

2 Heat the oil in the pan and fry the onion, garlic and allspice for 3 minutes. Stir in the ginger and rice and cook for 1 more minute.

3 Add the stock and bring to a boil. Reduce the heat, cover and simmer gently for 15 minutes, until the rice is just tender.

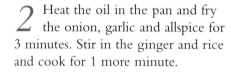

4 Stir in the saffron and liquid, the pine nuts, pickled walnuts, raisins and parsley or cilantro. Season to taste with salt and pepper. Heat through gently for 2 minutes. Garnish with parsley or cilantro leaves and serve with the soy yogurt.

NUTRITION NOTES	
Per portion:	
Calories	481
Protein	8.0g
Fat	25.8g
Saturated Fat	2.8g
Carbohydrate	57.7g
Fiber	1.3g
Iron	1.9mg
Calcium	62mg

VARIATION

Use one small eggplant, chopped and fried in a little olive oil, instead of the pickled walnuts, if desired.

1 Put the saffron in a bowl with 1 tablespoon boiling water and let stand. Heat a large frying pan and dry-fry the pine nuts until they turn golden. Set them aside.

Spicy Chickpea and Eggplant Stew

This is a Lebanese dish, but similar recipes are found all over the Mediterranean.

INGREDIENTS

Serves 6
3 large eggplant, cubed
1 cup chickpeas, soaked overnight
¼ cup olive oil
3 garlic cloves, chopped
2 large onions, chopped
½ teaspoon ground cumin
½ teaspoon ground cinnamon
½ teaspoon ground coriander
3 14-ounce cans chopped tomatoes
salt and freshly ground black pepper
cooked rice, to serve

For the garnish
2 tablespoons olive oil
1 onion, sliced
1 garlic clove, sliced
cilantro sprigs

1 Place the eggplant in a colander and sprinkle them with salt. Set the colander in a bowl and let sit for 30 minutes, to let the bitter juices escape. Rinse with cold water and pat dry with paper towels.

2 Drain the chickpeas and put in a large pan with enough water to cover. Bring to a boil and simmer for 30 minutes or until tender. Drain.

3 Heat the oil in a large pan. Add the garlic and onion and cook gently, until soft. Add the spices and cook, stirring, for a few seconds. Add the eggplant and stir to coat with the spices and onion. Cook for 5 minutes. Add the tomatoes and chickpeas and season. Cover and simmer for 20 minutes.

4 To make the garnish, heat the oil in a frying pan and add the sliced onion and garlic. Fry until golden and crisp. Serve the stew with rice, topped with the onion and garlic and garnished with sprigs of cilantro.

─── NUTRITION NOTES ───	
Per portion:	
Calories	261
Protein	10.2g
Fat	13.3g
Saturated Fat	1.8g
Carbohydrate	26.9g
Fiber	6.9g
Iron	3.0mg
Calcium	93.6mg

Mediterranean One-crust Pie

This free-form pie encases a rich tomato, eggplant and kidney bean filling. If your pastry cracks, just patch it up—it adds to the pie's rustic character.

INGREDIENTS

Serves 4

1¼ pounds eggplant, cubed
1 red bell pepper
2 tablespoons olive oil
1 large onion, finely chopped
1 zucchini, sliced
2 garlic cloves, crushed
1 tablespoon fresh oregano or
   1 teaspoon dried, plus extra fresh
   oregano to garnish
1½ cups canned red kidney beans,
   drained and rinsed
1 cup pitted black olives, rinsed
⅔ cup passata
2 tablespoons semolina
a little soy milk
salt and freshly ground black pepper

For the pastry
⅔ cup unbleached all-purpose flour
⅔ cup whole-wheat flour
6 tablespoons vegan margarine

1 Preheat the oven to 425°F. To make the pastry, rub the flours and fat together until the mixture resembles fine bread crumbs. Add enough cold water to form a dough.

2 Turn out the dough onto a lightly floured work surface and knead until smooth and elastic. Wrap in plastic wrap and chill for 30 minutes.

3 To make the filling, place the eggplant in a colander and sprinkle with salt, then let sit for 30 minutes. Rinse and pat dry with paper towels. Meanwhile, place the pepper on a baking sheet and roast in the oven for 20 minutes. Put the pepper in a plastic bag and let sit until cool enough to handle. Peel and seed the pepper, then dice the flesh. Set aside.

4 Heat the oil in a large heavy frying pan. Fry the onions for 5 minutes, until softened, stirring occasionally. Add the eggplant and fry for 5 minutes, until tender. Add the zucchini, garlic and oregano, and cook for another 5 minutes, stirring frequently. Add the kidney beans and olives, stir, then add the passata and pepper. Cook until heated through, and set aside to cool.

5 Roll out the pastry on a lightly floured board or work surface to form a rough 12-inch round. Place on a lightly oiled baking sheet. Sprinkle on the semolina, leaving a 1½-inch border, then spoon on the filling.

6 Gather up the edges of the pastry to partly cover the filling—it should be open in the middle. Brush with the soy milk and bake for 30–35 minutes, until golden.

NUTRITION NOTES	
Per portion:	
Calories	272
Protein	11.7g
Fat	25.8g
Saturated Fat	6.2g
Carbohydrate	51.5g
Fiber	10.5g
Iron	3.7mg
Calcium	125mg

Jamaican Black Bean Stew

INGREDIENTS

Serves 4

1¼ cups dried black beans
1 bay leaf
2 tablespoons vegetable oil
1 large onion, chopped
1 garlic clove, chopped
1 teaspoon English mustard powder
1 tablespoon molasses
2 tablespoons dark brown sugar
1 teaspoon dried thyme
½ teaspoon dried chile flakes
1 red bell pepper, seeded and diced
1 yellow bell pepper, seeded and diced
5¼ cups butternut squash or pumpkin,
    seeded and cut into ½-inch dice
salt and freshly ground black pepper
fresh thyme sprigs, to garnish

1 Soak the beans overnight in water, then drain and rinse. Place in a pan, cover with fresh water and add the bay leaf. Bring to a boil, then boil rapidly for 10 minutes. Reduce the heat, cover, and simmer for 30 minutes, until tender. Drain, reserving the cooking water. Preheat the oven to 350°F.

2 Heat the oil in the saucepan and sauté the onion and garlic for 5 minutes, until softened, stirring occasionally. Add the mustard powder, molasses, sugar, thyme and chile flakes and cook for 1 minute, stirring. Stir in the black beans and spoon the mixture into a flameproof casserole.

3 Add water to the reserved cooking liquid to make up 1⅔ cups, then pour into the casserole. Bake for 25 minutes.

4 Add the peppers and squash or pumpkin, season and mix well. Cover, then bake for 45 minutes, until the vegetables are tender. Serve garnished with fresh thyme sprigs.

--- COOK'S TIP ---

Molasses imparts a rich flavor to the spicy sauce. This dish is delicious served with cornbread or plain boiled rice.

--- NUTRITION NOTES ---

Per portion:

Calories	352
Protein	16.1g
Fat	6.8g
Saturated Fat	0.9g
Carbohydrate	60.7g
Fiber	8.9g
Iron	6.1mg
Calcium	150.3mg

Rice and Beans with Avocado Salsa

Mexican-style rice and beans make a delicious supper dish. Spoon onto tortillas and serve with a tangy avocado salsa. Alternatively, serve as a side dish with a spicy stew.

INGREDIENTS

Serves 4

¼ cup dried or ½ cup canned kidney
   beans, rinsed and drained
4 tomatoes, halved and seeded
2 garlic cloves, chopped
1 onion, sliced
3 tablespoons olive oil
generous 1 cup long-grain
   brown rice, rinsed
2½ cups vegetable stock
2 carrots, diced
¾ cup green beans
salt and freshly ground black pepper
4 wheat tortillas, to serve

For the avocado salsa

1 avocado
juice of 1 lime
1 small red onion, diced
1 small red chile, seeded and chopped
1 tablespoon chopped cilantro

1 If using dried kidney beans, place in a bowl, cover with cold water and let soak overnight, then drain and rinse well. Place in a saucepan with enough water to cover and bring to a boil. Boil rapidly for about 10 minutes, then reduce the heat and simmer for 40 minutes, until tender. Drain and set aside.

2 Preheat the broiler to high. Place the tomatoes, garlic and onion on a baking sheet. Pour on 1 tablespoon of the olive oil and toss to coat. Broil for 10 minutes or until the tomatoes and onions are softened, turning once. Set aside to cool.

3 Heat the remaining oil in a saucepan, add the rice and cook for 2 minutes, stirring, until light golden.

4 Purée the cooled tomatoes and onions in a food processor or blender, then add the mixture to the rice and cook for another 2 minutes, stirring frequently. Pour in the stock, then cover and cook gently, for 20 minutes, stirring occasionally.

5 Reserve 2 tablespoons of the kidney beans for the salsa. Add the rest to the stock mixture with the carrots and green beans and cook for 15 minutes, until the vegetables are tender. Season well. Remove the pan from heat and let stand, covered, for 15 minutes.

6 To make the avocado salsa, cut the avocado in half and remove the pit. Peel and dice the flesh, then toss in the lime juice. Add the onion, chile, cilantro and reserved kidney beans, then season with salt.

7 To serve, spoon hot rice and beans onto each of the tortillas. Pass the avocado salsa separately.

— NUTRITION NOTES —	
Per portion:	
Calories	397
Protein	6.8g
Fat	18.01g
Saturated Fat	3.2g
Carbohydrate	55.6g
Fiber	4.7g
Iron	2.1mg
Calcium	46.2mg

Creamy Leek and Mushroom Tagliatelle

INGREDIENTS

Serves 4
¼ cup olive oil
3 leeks, sliced into rounds
2 garlic cloves, chopped
3 cups button mushrooms, sliced
1 teaspoon dried oregano
½ teaspoon chile flakes
3 cups dried tagliatelle
5 tablespoons vegan cream cheese
2 tablespoons chopped fresh parsley,
   to garnish
salt and freshly ground black pepper

1 Heat the oil in a large heavy frying pan and sauté the leeks and garlic for 3 minutes, until soft. Add the mushrooms, oregano and chile flakes and cook gently for 5 more minutes until the mushrooms are tender.

2 Meanwhile, cook the tagliatelle in a large pan of salted boiling water for 8-12 minutes until al dente. Drain, reserving ¼ cup of the cooking water for the mushroom mixture.

3 Stir the reserved cooking water into the mushroom mixture, then add the cream cheese and season. Heat gently for 1-2 minutes, stirring occasionally.

4 To serve, spoon the sauce on the tagliatelle and sprinkle with chopped fresh parsley.

NUTRITION NOTES	
Per portion:	
Calories	534
Protein	14.6g
Fat	22.5g
Saturated Fat	7.54g
Carbohydrate	73.0g
Fiber	5.3g
Iron	4.0mg
Calcium	87mg

Dairy-free Pesto with Spirali

INGREDIENTS

Serves 4
11 ounces new potatoes, cubed
1 cup green beans, cut into thirds
8 ounces broccoli florets
3 cups dried spirali pasta
2 tomatoes, seeded and diced
¼ cup pine nuts, toasted
salt and freshly ground black pepper

For the pesto
1 ounce fresh basil leaves, torn
¼ ounce fresh mint leaves, torn
2 large garlic cloves, crushed
1 tablespoon Dijon mustard
¼ cup pine nuts
¼ cup extra virgin olive oil
juice of ½ lemon

1 To make the pesto, purée the basil and mint, garlic, mustard, pine nuts, oil and lemon juice in a food processor or blender. Season and set aside.

2 Cook the new potatoes in a large pan of salted boiling water for 5-7 minutes, until just tender. Steam the green beans and broccoli for 3 minutes, until they are tender.

NUTRITION NOTES	
Per portion:	
Calories	610
Protein	18.5g
Fat	22.7g
Saturated Fat	2.78g
Carbohydrate	88.4g
Fiber	6.7g
Iron	4.8mg
Calcium	101mg

3 Cook the spirali in a large pan of salted boiling water for 10-12 minutes until al dente. Drain, reserving ⅔ cup of the cooking water. Return the pasta and reserved water to the pan. Add the precooked potatoes, beans, broccoli, pesto and seasoning, then stir until combined. Heat over low heat for 1-2 minutes, then stir in the tomatoes. Serve sprinkled with toasted pine nuts.

Stuffed Tomatoes and Bell Peppers

Colorful bell peppers and tomatoes make perfect containers for filling with various vegetable and grain stuffings. This rice and herb version uses typically Greek ingredients.

INGREDIENTS

Serves 4
2 large ripe tomatoes
1 green bell pepper
1 yellow or orange bell pepper
¼ cup olive oil, plus extra
   for sprinkling
2 onions, chopped
2 garlic cloves, crushed
½ cup blanched almonds, chopped
scant ½ cup long-grain rice, boiled
   and drained
½ ounce fresh mint, roughly chopped
½ ounce fresh parsley, roughly chopped
2 tablespoons golden raisins
3 tablespoons ground almonds
salt and freshly ground black pepper
chopped mixed fresh herbs, to garnish

1 Preheat the oven to 375°F. Cut the tomatoes in half and scoop out the pulp and seeds using a teaspoon. Let the tomatoes drain on paper towels with cut-sides down. Roughly chop the tomato pulp and seeds.

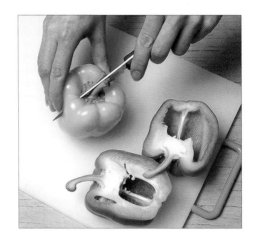

2 Halve the peppers, leaving the cores intact. Scoop out the seeds. Brush the peppers with 1 tablespoon of the oil and bake on a baking sheet for 15 minutes. Place the peppers and tomatoes in a shallow ovenproof dish and season with salt and pepper.

3 Fry the onions in the remaining oil for 5 minutes. Add the garlic and chopped almonds and fry for another minute.

4 Remove the pan from heat and stir in the rice, the insides of the chopped tomatoes, mint, parsley and golden raisins. Season well with salt and pepper, then spoon the mixture into the tomatoes and peppers.

5 Pour ⅔ cup boiling water around the tomatoes and peppers and bake, uncovered, for 20 minutes. Sprinkle on the ground almonds and sprinkle with a little extra olive oil. Return to the oven and bake for another 20 minutes or until turning golden. Serve garnished with fresh herbs.

— NUTRITION NOTES —	
Per portion:	
Calories	370
Protein	7.9g
Fat	25.4g
Saturated Fat	2.9g
Carbohydrate	29.4g
Fiber	4.1g
Iron	1.6mg
Calcium	87.7mg

— VARIATION —

Small eggplant or large zucchini also make good vegetables for stuffing. Halve and scoop out the centers of the vegetables, then oil the vegetable shells and bake for about 15 minutes. Chop the centers, fry for 2–3 minutes to soften and add to the stuffing mixture. Fill the eggplant or zucchini shells with the stuffing and bake as for the peppers and tomatoes.

Caramelized Red Onion and Thyme Tart

This flavorful tart is perfect for a light summer lunch. Serve with green beans tossed in a vinaigrette dressing, and warm new potatoes.

INGREDIENTS

Serves 6
1½ tablespoons olive oil
3 medium red onions, finely sliced
1 teaspoon dried thyme
½ teaspoon brown sugar
3½ ounces silken tofu
⅔ cup soy cream
1 tablespoon Dijon mustard
salt and freshly ground black pepper

For the pastry
1 ¼ cups whole-wheat self-rising flour
5 tablespoons vegan margarine
¼ cup walnuts, finely chopped
pinch of salt

1 For the pastry, sift the whole-wheat flour and salt into a bowl, adding any bran left in the sieve. Rub in the margarine with your fingers until the mixture resembles fine bread crumbs. Mix in the walnuts, then add enough cold water to form a dough.

2 Turn out the dough onto a lightly floured work surface and knead until smooth and elastic. Wrap in plastic wrap and chill for 30 minutes.

3 Meanwhile make the onion and thyme filling. Heat the oil in a large heavy frying pan. Sweat the onions over low heat for 20 minutes until very soft and translucent, stirring often. Stir in the thyme, sugar and seasoning and cook for another 5 minutes until caramelized. Set aside to cool slightly.

4 Blend the silken tofu, soy cream, Dijon mustard and seasoning in a food processor or blender until smooth and creamy.

COOK'S TIP

It is important to cook the onions very gently over low heat so that they remain soft and succulent. If preferred, the pastry shell can be prepared in advance. Bake it blind for 10 minutes, and keep in an airtight container for up to 2 days.

5 Preheat the oven to 400°F. Lightly grease a fluted 9-inch loose-bottomed tart pan. Roll out the pastry on a lightly floured work surface, then gently lift it using a rolling pin and line the prepared pan. Press the pastry into the pan with your finger tips and trim the top. Chill for another 20 minutes.

6 Prick the pastry shell with a fork, line with waxed paper and baking beans and bake blind for 10 minutes until lightly golden. Remove the paper and beans, then spoon on the onions. Spoon in the tofu mixture and smooth with a knife. Bake for 30 minutes, until golden and set.

NUTRITION NOTES

Per portion:

Calories	301
Protein	7.1g
Fat	20.7g
Saturated Fat	3.93g
Carbohydrate	22.8g
Fiber	3.3g
Iron	1.8mg
Calcium	170mg

SALADS AND SIDE DISHES

This group of versatile recipes puts the focus on flavor and simplicity,

with a choice of salads and side dishes that are light enough to serve

with vegan whole-food main courses or to enjoy on their own for a

light lunch or supper. Simple salad ingredients are given a twist with

special dressings, and cooked vegetables are assembled in colorful

composed salads with inspirational results.

Japanese Salad

Hijiki is a mild-tasting seaweed, and combined with radishes, cucumber and bean sprouts, it makes a refreshing salad, ideal to serve with a noodle dish.

INGREDIENTS

Serves 4
½ cup hijiki
1¼ cups radishes, sliced
1 small cucumber, cut into thin sticks
½ cup bean sprouts

For the dressing
1 tablespoon sunflower oil
1 tablespoon sesame oil
1 teaspoon light soy sauce
2 tablespoons rice vinegar or
   1 tablespoon wine vinegar
1 tablespoon mirin

1 Soak the hijiki in a bowl of cold water for 10–15 minutes, until rehydrated. Drain, rinse under cold running water and drain again. The hijiki should almost triple in volume.

2 Place the hijiki in a saucepan of water. Bring to a boil, then reduce the heat and simmer for about 30 minutes or until tender.

3 Meanwhile, make the dressing. Place the sunflower and sesame oils, soy sauce, vinegar and mirin in a bowl or screw-top jar. Stir or shake thoroughly to combine.

4 Arrange the hijiki in a shallow bowl or platter with the radishes, cucumber and bean sprouts. Pour on the dressing and toss lightly.

— NUTRITION NOTES —	
Per portion:	
Calories	68
Protein	1.7g
Fat	5.8g
Saturated Fat	0.8g
Carbohydrate	2.4g
Fiber	2.8g
Iron	1.2mg
Calcium	46mg

Moroccan Date, Orange and Carrot Salad

A colorful and unusual salad, made with exotic ingredients.

INGREDIENTS

Serves 4

1 head Boston lettuce
2 carrots, finely grated
2 oranges
4 ounces fresh dates, stoned and cut
  into eighths, lengthwise
¼ cup toasted whole almonds, chopped
2 tablespoons lemon juice
1 teaspoon sugar
¼ teaspoon salt
1 tablespoon orange flower water

1 Separate the lettuce leaves and arrange them in the bottom of a salad bowl or on individual serving plates. Place the grated carrot in a mound on top.

— NUTRITION NOTES —

Per portion:

Calories	115
Protein	3.0g
Fat	3.8g
Saturated Fat	0.3g
Carbohydrate	18.2g
Fiber	3.3g
Iron	0.6mg
Calcium	76.5mg

2 Peel and segment the oranges and arrange them around the carrot. Pile the dates on top, then sprinkle on the almonds. Combine the lemon juice, sugar, salt and orange flower water and sprinkle on the salad. Serve chilled.

Warm Vegetable Salad with Peanut Sauce

INGREDIENTS

Serves 4
8 new potatoes
8 ounces broccoli
1½ cups green beans
2 carrots
1 red bell pepper, seeded and cut
 into strips
½ cup sprouted beans
sprigs of watercress, to garnish

For the peanut sauce
1 tablespoon sunflower oil
1 bird's eye chile, seeded and sliced
1 garlic clove, crushed
1 teaspoon ground coriander
1 teaspoon ground cumin
¼ cup crunchy peanut butter
5 tablespoons water
1 tablespoon dark soy sauce
½-inch piece fresh ginger root,
 finely grated
1 teaspoon dark brown sugar
1 tablespoon lime juice
¼ cup coconut milk

1 First, make the peanut sauce. Heat the oil in a saucepan, add the chile and garlic, and cook for 1 minute or until softened. Add the spices and cook for 1 minute. Stir in the peanut butter and water, then cook for 2 minutes, until combined, stirring constantly.

2 Add the soy sauce, ginger, sugar, lime juice and coconut milk, then cook over low heat until the mixture is smooth and heated through, stirring frequently. Transfer to a bowl.

3 Bring a large saucepan of salted water to a boil, add the potatoes and cook for 10–15 minutes, until tender. Drain, then halve or thickly slice the potatoes, depending on their size.

4 Meanwhile, trim the broccoli stems and cut into small florets. Cut the carrots into thin ribbons using a vegetable peeler. Place the broccoli in a steamer with the green beans and steam for 4–5 minutes, until tender but still crisp. Add the carrots to the steamer 2 minutes before the end of the cooking time.

5 Arrange the cooked vegetables on a serving platter with the red bell pepper and sprouted beans. Garnish with watercress, and serve with the peanut sauce passed separately.

---- COOK'S TIP ----

This recipe will serve four as a side dish, or it will serve two as a main course for lunch or supper.

---- NUTRITION NOTES ----

Per portion:

Calories	206
Protein	9.5g
Fat	8.9g
Saturated Fat	1.7g
Carbohydrate	23.3g
Fiber	6.4g
Iron	3.8mg
Calcium	89mg

Roasted Plum Tomatoes with Garlic

This light salad is simple to prepare, and tastes absolutely wonderful. Use a shallow earthenware dish that will allow the tomatoes to sear and char in the hot oven.

INGREDIENTS

Serves 4
8 plum tomatoes, halved
12 garlic cloves, unpeeled
¼ cup extra virgin olive oil
3 bay leaves
3 tablespoons fresh oregano leaves,
　to garnish
salt and freshly ground black pepper

1 Preheat the oven to 450°F. Select an ovenproof dish that will hold all the tomatoes snugly in a single layer. Place the tomatoes in the dish and push the whole garlic cloves between them.

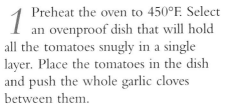

2 Brush the tomatoes with oil, add the bay leaves and sprinkle with pepper. Bake for 45 minutes, until the tomatoes have softened and are sizzling in the pan. They should be charred around the edges. Season with salt and a little more pepper, if needed. Garnish with fresh oregano and serve.

NUTRITION NOTES	
Per portion:	
Calories	147
Protein	2.5g
Fat	11.7g
Saturated Fat	1.6g
Carbohydrate	8.4g
Fiber	2.3g
Iron	1.2mg
Calcium	38mg

Monk-style Mixed Vegetables

Chinese monks eat neither meat
nor fish, so "Monk-style" dishes
are ideal for vegans.

INGREDIENTS

Serves 4
2 ounces dried tofu sticks
4 ounces fresh lotus root, or
  2 ounces dried lotus root
¼ ounce dried wood ears
8 dried Chinese mushrooms
1 tablespoon vegetable oil
¾ cup drained, canned
  straw mushrooms
1 cup baby corn, cut in half
2 tablespoons light soy sauce
1 tablespoon dry sherry
2 teaspoons sugar
⅔ cup vegetable stock
3 ounces snowpeas, trimmed and
  cut in half
1 teaspoon cornstarch
1 tablespoon water
salt

2 Prepare the wood ears and dried
Chinese mushrooms by soaking
them in separate bowls of hot water
for 15 minutes. Drain the wood ears,
trim off and discard the hard base from
each and cut the rest into bite-size
pieces. Drain the soaked mushrooms,
trim off and discard the stems and
chop the caps roughly.

3 Drain the tofu sticks. Cut them
into 2-inch long pieces, discarding
any hard parts. If using dried lotus
root, drain well.

4 Heat the oil in a frying pan or
wok. Stir-fry the wood ears,
Chinese mushrooms and lotus root
for about 30 seconds

5 Add the pieces of tofu sticks,
straw mushrooms, baby corn,
soy sauce, sherry, sugar and stock.
Bring to a boil, then cover the pan or
wok, lower the heat and simmer for
about 20 minutes.

6 Stir in the snowpeas, with salt to
taste and cook, uncovered, for
2 more minutes. Mix the cornstarch
to a paste with the water. Add the
mixture to the pan or wok. Cook,
stirring, until the sauce thickens.
Serve immediately.

1 Put the tofu sticks in a bowl.
Cover with hot water and let soak
for 1 hour. If using fresh lotus root,
peel it and slice it; if using dried lotus
root, place it in a bowl of hot water
and let soak for 1 hour.

——— NUTRITION NOTES ———	
Per portion:	
Calories	73
Protein	4.6g
Fat	4.2g
Saturated Fat	0.5g
Carbohydrate	4.7g
Fiber	2.0g
Iron	1.2mg
Calcium	87.2mg

Couscous Salad

This is a spicy variation on the classic tabbouleh salad, which is traditionally made with bulghur wheat, not couscous.

INGREDIENTS

Serves 4
3 tablespoons olive oil
5 scallions, chopped
1 garlic clove, crushed
1 teaspoon ground cumin
1½ cups vegetable stock
1 cup couscous
2 tomatoes, peeled and chopped
¼ cup chopped fresh parsley
¼ cup chopped fresh mint
1 fresh green chile, seeded and
    finely chopped
2 tablespoons lemon juice
salt and freshly ground black pepper
toasted pine nuts and grated lemon
    zest, to garnish
crisp lettuce leaves, to serve

1 Heat the oil in a saucepan. Add the scallions and garlic. Stir in the cumin and cook for 1 minute. Add the stock and bring to a boil.

2 Remove the pan from heat, stir in the couscous, cover the pan and let stand for 10 minutes, until the couscous has swelled and all the liquid has been absorbed. If using instant couscous, follow the instructions on the package.

3 Transfer the couscous to a bowl. Stir in the tomatoes, parsley, mint, chile and lemon juice, with salt and pepper to taste. If possible, let stand for up to an hour to let the flavors develop.

4 To serve, line a bowl with crisp lettuce leaves and spoon the couscous salad into the center. Sprinkle on the toasted pine nuts and grated lemon zest, to garnish.

NUTRITION NOTES	
Per portion:	
Calories	185
Protein	3.2g
Fat	8.9g
Saturated Fat	1.2g
Carbohydrate	24.4g
Fiber	0.6g
Iron	3.1mg
Calcium	26mg

Broccoli with Soy Sauce

A wonderfully simple dish that you will want to make again and again. The broccoli cooks in minutes, so don't start cooking until you are almost ready to eat.

INGREDIENTS

Serves 4
1 pound broccoli
1 tablespoon vegetable oil
2 garlic cloves, crushed
2 tablespoons light soy sauce
salt
fried garlic slices, to garnish

1 Trim the thick stems of the broccoli and cut the head into large florets.

2 Bring a large saucepan of salted water to a boil. Add the broccoli and cook for 3–4 minutes, until crisp and tender.

3 Drain the broccoli, arrange in a serving dish and keep warm.

4 Heat the oil in a small saucepan. Fry the garlic for 2 minutes to release the flavor, then remove it with a slotted spoon. Pour the hot oil carefully over the broccoli, being careful as it will splatter. Drizzle the soy sauce on the broccoli, sprinkle on the fried garlic and serve.

NUTRITION NOTES	
Per portion:	
Calories	61
Protein	4.9g
Fat	3.8g
Saturated Fat	0.5g
Carbohydrate	2.0g
Fiber	2.9g
Iron	1.9mg
Calcium	63mg

Glazed Sweet Potatoes with Ginger and Allspice

Fried sweet potatoes acquire a candied coating when cooked with ginger, syrup and allspice. Cayenne pepper cuts through the sweetness.

INGREDIENTS

Serves 4
2 pounds sweet potatoes
2 tablespoons vegan margarine
3 tablespoons olive oil
2 garlic cloves, crushed
2 pieces of crystallized ginger, roughly chopped
2 teaspoons ground allspice
1 tablespoon syrup from crystallized ginger jar
2 teaspoons chopped fresh thyme, plus extra sprigs to garnish
salt and cayenne pepper

1 Peel the sweet potatoes and cut into ½-inch cubes. Melt the margarine with the oil in a frying pan. Add the sweet potato cubes and fry for 10 minutes, until just soft.

——— NUTRITION NOTES ———	
Per portion:	
Calories	327
Protein	2.7g
Fat	14.0g
Saturated Fat	2.9g
Carbohydrate	50.9g
Fiber	5.4g
Iron	1.6mg
Calcium	54.7mg

2 Stir in the garlic, ginger and allspice. Cook, stirring, for 5 more minutes. Stir in the ginger syrup, salt, a generous pinch of cayenne pepper and the fresh thyme. Stir for 1–2 more minutes, then serve sprinkled with thyme sprigs.

Roasted Root Vegetables with Whole Spice Seeds

These spicy root vegetables are delicious served as the main part of a meal with rice or couscous, or as a side dish.

INGREDIENTS

Serves 4
3 parsnips, peeled
3 potatoes, peeled
3 carrots, peeled
3 sweet potatoes, peeled
¼ cup olive oil
8 shallots, peeled
2 garlic cloves, sliced
2 teaspoons white mustard seeds
2 teaspoons coriander seeds, lightly crushed
1 teaspoon cumin seeds
2 bay leaves
salt and ground black pepper

1 Preheat the oven to 375°F. Bring a saucepan of lightly salted water to a boil. Cut the parsnips, potatoes, carrots and sweet potatoes into chunks. Add them to the pan and bring the water back to a boil. Boil for 2 minutes, then drain the vegetables thoroughly.

2 Pour the olive oil into a large heavy roasting pan and place over medium heat. Add the vegetables, shallots and garlic. Fry, tossing the vegetables over the heat until they are pale golden at the edges.

3 Add the mustard seeds, coriander seeds, cumin seeds and bay leaves. Cook for 1 minute, then season to taste with salt and pepper. Transfer the roasting pan to the oven and roast for 45 minutes, turning occasionally, until the vegetables are crisp and golden and cooked through.

——— VARIATION ———
Vary the selection of vegetables according to what is available. Try using rutabaga or pumpkin instead of, or as well as, the vegetables suggested here.

——— NUTRITION NOTES ———	
Per portion:	
Calories	234
Protein	3.4g
Fat	12.1g
Saturated Fat	1.8g
Carbohydrate	29.5g
Fiber	4.6g
Iron	0.9mg
Calcium	45mg

Rice with Dill and Fava Beans

This is a favorite rice dish in Iran, where it is called *baghali polo*. The combination of fava beans, dill and warm spices works very well, and the saffron rice adds a splash of bright color.

INGREDIENTS

Serves 4

1½ cups basmati rice, soaked
3 cups water
3 tablespoons melted vegan margarine
1½ cups frozen baby fava beans, thawed and peeled
6 tablespoons finely chopped fresh dill, plus 1 fresh dill sprig, to garnish
1 teaspoon ground cinnamon
1 teaspoon ground cumin
2–3 saffron threads, soaked in 1 tablespoon boiling water
salt

1 Drain the rice, put it into a pan and pour in the measured water. Add a little salt. Bring to a boil, then lower the heat and simmer very gently for 10 minutes. Drain, rinse in warm water and drain once again.

2 Melt the margarine in a nonstick saucepan. Pour two-thirds of the melted margarine into a small bowl and set aside. Spoon enough rice into the pan to cover the bottom. Add a quarter of the beans and a little dill. Spread on another layer of rice, then a layer of beans and dill. Repeat the layers until all the beans and dill have been used up, ending with a layer of rice. Cook over low heat for 8 minutes, until nearly tender.

3 Pour the reserved melted margarine over the rice. Sprinkle with the ground cinnamon and cumin. Cover the pan with a clean dish towel and a tight-fitting lid, lifting the corners of the cloth back over the lid. Cook over low heat for 25–30 minutes.

4 Spoon about 3 tablespoons of the cooked rice into the bowl of saffron water; mix well. Mound the remaining rice mixture on a large serving plate and spoon the saffron rice on one side to decorate. Serve immediately, decorated with a sprig of fresh dill.

NUTRITION NOTES	
Per portion:	
Calories	346
Protein	76g
Fat	8.9g
Saturated Fat	2.5g
Carbohydrate	58g
Fiber	2.6g
Iron	1.3mg
Calcium	23.5mg

Mushroom Pilaf

This dish is simplicity itself. Serve with an Indian vegetable or lentil dish and warmed naan.

INGREDIENTS

Serves 4
3 tablespoons vegetable oil
2 shallots, finely chopped
1 garlic clove, crushed
3 green cardamom pods
2¼ cups button mushrooms, sliced
generous 1 cup basmati rice, soaked
1 teaspoon grated fresh ginger root
good pinch of garam masala
scant 2 cups water
1 tablespoon chopped cilantro
salt

1 Heat the oil in a flameproof casserole and fry the shallots, garlic and cardamom pods over medium heat for 3–4 minutes, until the shallots have softened and are beginning to brown.

2 Add the mushrooms and fry for 2–3 more minutes. Add the rice, ginger and garam masala. Stir-fry over low heat for 2 minutes, then stir in the water and salt. Bring to a boil, cover and simmer for 10 minutes.

3 Remove the casserole from heat. Let stand, covered, for 5 minutes. Add the chopped cilantro and fork it through the rice. Spoon into a serving bowl and serve immediately.

NUTRITION NOTES	
Per portion:	
Calories	285
Protein	5.1g
Fat	8.7g
Saturated Fat	0.9g
Carbohydrate	45.7g
Fiber	0.5g
Iron	1.0mg
Calcium	15.7mg

DESSERTS

This collection is proof that you don't need to be a dairy food eater to enjoy elaborate desserts. Simple poached fruit on its own is all that some menus need as a sweetener, but for occasions where a touch of luxury is needed, choose from one of the sensational vegan desserts included here. Sorbets, ice creams, cheesecakes, crumbles and fruit tarts are all easily achievable using soy milk products in place of dairy milk, cream and eggs.

Strawberry and Vanilla Tofu Ice

This pretty pink dairy-free ice cream has a remarkably creamy taste. Serve with slices of fresh strawberry, or in a cone, drizzled with strawberry syrup.

Ingredients

Serves 8
scant 2 cups soy milk
¼ cup sugar
4 teaspoons cornstarch
1 teaspoon vanilla extract
1¼ pounds silken tofu
1 tablespoon sunflower oil
2 tablespoons maple syrup
2 cups strawberries, hulled and halved

1 Reserve ¼ cup soy milk, then pour the remainder into a large saucepan, and bring to a boil. Blend the sugar and cornstarch with the reserved milk in a bowl. Add the sugar mixture and vanilla extract to the warm milk. Simmer, stirring, for 2 minutes, until thickened.

2 Pour the mixture into a bowl, cover with a sheet of waxed paper to prevent a skin forming, then let cool.

3 Blend the silken tofu, sunflower oil, maple syrup and strawberries, reserving a few of the best ones to decorate, in a food processor or blender until smooth and creamy.

4 Add the strawberry mixture to the cooled custard and mix to combine. Pour the mixture into a freezerproof container and freeze for 2 hours.

5 Whisk the half-frozen mixture until smooth, then return to the freezer for another hour. Whisk again and freeze until solid. Remove the ice cream from the freezer 20 minutes before serving to let it soften.

NUTRITION NOTES	
Per portion:	
Calories	135
Protein	7.0g
Fat	5.4g
Saturated Fat	0.73g
Carbohydrate	15.3g
Fiber	0.3g
Iron	1.8mg
Calcium	365mg

VARIATION

Substitute the strawberries with raspberries, mango or peaches, if desired.

Chocolate Sorbet with Berries

The chill that thrills, that's chocolate sorbet. For a really fine texture, it helps to have an ice cream maker, which churns the mixture as it freezes, but you can make it by hand quite easily.

INGREDIENTS

Serves 6
2 cups water
3 tablespoons maple syrup
generous ½ cup sugar
¾ cup unsweetened cocoa powder
2 ounces bittersweet chocolate, broken into squares
14 ounces soft red fruits, such as raspberries, red currants or strawberries, to serve

1 Place the water, maple syrup, sugar and cocoa powder in a saucepan. Heat gently, stirring occasionally, until the sugar has completely dissolved.

2 Remove from heat, add the chocolate and stir until melted. Let sit until cool.

COOK'S TIP

This sorbet looks attractive if served in small oval scoops shaped with two spoons. Simply scoop out the sorbet with one tablespoon, then use another to smooth it off and transfer to a plate.

3 Transfer to an ice cream maker and churn until frozen. Alternatively, pour into a freezer-proof container and freeze until slushy, then whisk until smooth and freeze again for another hour. Whisk again and freeze until solid.

4 Remove from the freezer 10–15 minutes before serving, so that the sorbet softens slightly. Serve in scoops, with the berries.

NUTRITION NOTES	
Per portion:	
Calories	199
Protein	3.6g
Fat	5.2g
Saturated Fat	2.94g
Carbohydrate	36.6g
Fiber	3.7g
Iron	2.3mg
Calcium	57mg

Pears with Ginger and Star Anise

Star anise and ginger give a refreshing twist to this traditional recipe for poached pears. Serve slightly chilled, with soy yogurt.

Ingredients

serves 4

6 tablespoons sugar
1¼ cups white dessert wine
thinly pared zest and juice of
  1 lemon
3-inch piece of fresh ginger
  root, bruised
5 star anise
10 cloves
2½ cups water
6 slightly unripe pears
3 tablespoons drained, crystallized
  ginger in syrup, sliced
thick soy yogurt, to serve

1 Place the sugar, dessert wine, lemon zest and juice, ginger, star anise, cloves and water into a saucepan just large enough to hold the pears snugly in an upright position. Bring to a boil.

2 Meanwhile, peel the pears, leaving the stems intact. Add them to the wine mixture, making sure that they are totally immersed in the liquid.

3 Return the wine mixture to a boil, lower the heat, cover and simmer for 15–20 minutes or until the pears are tender. Lift out the pears with a slotted spoon and place them in a heatproof dish. Boil the wine syrup rapidly until it is reduced by about half, then pour over the pears. Let them cool, then chill.

4 Cut the pears into thick slices and arrange these on four serving plates. Remove the ginger and whole spices from the wine sauce, stir in the preserved ginger and spoon the sauce over the pears. Serve with soy yogurt.

NUTRITION NOTES	
Per portion:	
Calories	190
Protein	0.9g
Fat	0.3g
Saturated Fat	0.0g
Carbohydrate	45.2g
Fiber	5.3g
Iron	0.7mg
Calcium	32mg

Tapioca and Taro Pudding

This pudding is light and surprisingly refreshing, and is popular with children and adults alike. Serve it warm or chilled.

INGREDIENTS

Serves 4–6
⅔ cup tapioca
6¼ cups water
8 ounces taro
⅔ cup rock sugar
1¼ cups coconut milk

1 Rinse and drain the tapioca, then place in a bowl with fresh water to cover. Let soak for 30 minutes.

2 Drain the tapioca and put it in a saucepan with 3¾ cups water. Bring to a boil, then lower the heat and simmer for about 6 minutes or until the tapioca is transparent. Drain, refresh under cold water, and drain again.

3 Peel the taro and cut it into diamond-shaped slices, about ½-inch thick. Pour the remaining water into a saucepan and bring it to a boil. Add the taro and cook for 10–15 minutes or until it is just tender.

4 Using a slotted spoon, lift out half of the taro slices and set them aside. Continue to cook the remaining taro until it is very soft, then transfer the taro and cooking liquid to a food processor or blender and process until completely smooth.

5 Return the taro "soup" to the clean pan; stir in the sugar and simmer, stirring occasionally, until the sugar has dissolved.

6 Stir in the tapioca, reserved taro and coconut milk. Cook for a few minutes. Serve immediately in heated bowls. Alternatively, cool and chill before serving.

--- COOK'S TIP ---
Taro is a starchy tuber that tastes a lot like a baking potato. If it is difficult to obtain, use sweet potato instead.

--- NUTRITION NOTES ---
Per portion (if serving 4):

Calories	457
Protein	0.6g
Fat	0.3g
Saturated Fat	0.2g
Carbohydrate	122g
Fiber	0.9g
Iron	0.3g
Calcium	49.5mg

Tropical Mango and Pecan Cheesecake

This cheesecake is so rich and creamy, it is hard to believe it's completely dairy-free. Sometimes it's nice to be naughty!

INGREDIENTS

Serves 8
5 tablespoons vegan margarine
½ cup vegan oat cookies, crushed
¼ cup ground almonds
1 large mango, diced
juice of 1 lemon
scant 1 cup natural soy yogurt
1 tablespoon cornstarch
3 tablespoons maple syrup
2 8-ounce tubs vegan cream cheese

For the topping
½ cup shelled pecans
2 tablespoons maple syrup
1 mango, diced

2 Meanwhile, blend the mango, lemon juice, yogurt, cornstarch, maple syrup and vegan cream cheese in a food processor until smooth. Pour the mixture over the cookie crust and smooth with the back of a spoon. Bake for 25–30 minutes, until lightly golden and set. Let cool in the pan, then transfer to a wire rack and refrigerate until ready to serve.

4 Arrange the pecans around the edge of the cheesecake, reserving a few to decorate the center. Arrange the mango inside the outer circle of nuts. Pour on any remaining maple syrup.

NUTRITION NOTES	
Per portion:	
Calories	589
Protein	6.6g
Fat	47.7g
Saturated Fat	20.34g
Carbohydrate	35.4g
Fiber	2.9g
Iron	1.7mg
Calcium	108mg

COOK'S TIP

Vegan cream cheese is now widely available at health food stores. It is usually a mixture of soy and vegetable oils.

1 Preheat the oven to 350°F. To make the cheesecake crust, melt the margarine in a saucepan, then stir in the crushed cookies and ground almonds. Press the crumb mixture into the bottom of a deep, lightly greased 9-inch springform pan. Cook in the preheated oven for 10 minutes.

3 To make the topping, toast the pecans in a dry frying pan for 2-3 minutes until browned. Heat the maple syrup in a separate pan, then add to the pecans in the frying pan. Stir well to coat. Remove from heat and brush the top of the cheesecake with the maple syrup.

Orange Blossom Gelatin

A fresh orange gelatin makes a delightful dessert. The natural fruit flavor combined with the smooth texture has a cleansing quality that is especially welcome after a rich main course. Serve with thin crisp cookies.

INGREDIENTS

Serves 4–6
5 tablespoons sugar
⅔ cup water
3 heaping teaspoons vegetable
  gelatin powder
2½ cups freshly squeezed orange juice
2 tablespoons orange flower water

1 Place the sugar and water in a small saucepan and gently heat to dissolve the sugar. Let cool.

2 Sprinkle on the vegetable gelatin powder and mix well until it is incorporated.

3 Add the orange juice to the saucepan, then bring the mixture to a boil. Reduce the heat, and remove the pan as soon as the liquid begins to thicken.

4 Wet a gelatin mold and pour in the gelatin. Chill for at least 2 hours or until set. Turn out onto a serving plate, and decorate with fresh flowers, if desired.

—— COOK'S TIP ——

Vegetable gelatin powder contains carrageen, a seaweed that has similar setting properties to the animal-derived gelatin. Agar-agar is another seaweed that can be used in place of carrageen and is available in strips or flakes. Substitute 1 teaspoon agar-agar flakes for the vegetable gelatin powder in this recipe, if desired.

—— NUTRITION NOTES ——

Per portion (if serving 4):

Calories	135
Protein	5.1g
Fat	0.0g
Saturated Fat	0.0g
Carbohydrate	30.5g
Fiber	0.2g
Iron	0.6mg
Calcium	37mg

Mixed Berry Tart

The orange-flavored pastry is delicious with the creamy filling and fresh summer berries. Decorate this tart with finely shredded orange zest and serve with vanilla soy ice cream.

INGREDIENTS

Serves 8

For the pastry
2 cups unbleached all-purpose flour
½ cup vegan margarine
finely grated zest of 1 orange,
    plus extra to decorate

For the filling
1¼ cups thick soy yogurt
finely grated zest of 1 lemon
2 teaspoons confectioners' sugar
1½ pounds mixed berries

1 To make the pastry, sift the flour into a bowl. Add the margarine and rub with your fingers until the mixture resembles fine bread crumbs. Add the orange zest and enough cold water to make a soft dough.

2 Knead the dough on a lightly floured work surface until smooth and elastic, then form into a ball, wrap in plastic wrap and chill for 30 minutes.

3 Roll out the pastry and use to line a 9-inch loose-bottomed fluted tart pan. Chill for 30 minutes. Preheat the oven to 400°F and place a baking sheet in the oven to heat up.

4 Line the pastry with waxed paper and baking beans, place on the heated baking sheet and bake blind for 15 minutes. Remove the paper and beans, and bake for 10 more minutes, until golden. Let cool completely.

5 To make the filling, whisk together the soy yogurt, lemon zest and sugar, then spoon the mixture evenly into the pastry shell. Top with the mixed berries and sprinkle with the reserved orange zest. Serve the tart with spoonfuls of vanilla soy ice cream.

NUTRITION NOTES

Per portion:

Calories	255
Protein	5.5g
Fat	13.8g
Saturated Fat	4.06g
Carbohydrate	29.1g
Fiber	2.7g
Iron	1.2mg
Calcium	64mg

Blackberry Charlotte

A classic pudding, perfect for chilly autumn days. Serve with thick soy cream or a homemade vegan custard.

INGREDIENTS

Serves 4

5 tablespoons vegan margarine
3 cups fresh white bread crumbs
¼ cup brown sugar
¼ cup light corn syrup
finely grated zest and juice of
  2 lemons
2 ounces walnut halves
1 pound blackberries
1 pound apples, peeled, cored
  and finely sliced

1 Preheat the oven to 350°F. Grease a scant 2-cup dish with 1 tablespoon of the margarine. Melt the remaining margarine and add the bread crumbs. Sauté for 5–7 minutes, until the crumbs are crisp and golden. Let cool slightly.

2 Place the sugar, syrup, lemon zest and juice in a small saucepan and gently warm them. Add the crumbs.

3 Process the walnut halves until they are finely ground.

4 Arrange a thin layer of blackberries in the bottom of the dish. Top with a thin layer of crumbs.

5 Add a thin layer of apple, topping it with another thin layer of crumbs. Repeat the process with another layer of blackberries, followed by a layer of crumbs. Continue until you have used up all the ingredients, finishing with a layer of crumbs. The mixture should be piled well above the top of the dish because it shrinks during cooking. Bake for 30 minutes, until the crumbs are golden and the fruit is soft. Serve warm.

NUTRITION NOTES	
Per portion:	
Calories	484
Protein	7.0g
Fat	23.0g
Saturated Fat	5.6g
Carbohydrate	66.5g
Fiber	6.4g
Iron	2.3mg
Calcium	126mg

Rhubarb and Orange Crumble

This tangy fruit crumble is extra delicious with homemade dairy-free custard. The almonds give the crumble topping a nutty taste and crunchy texture.

INGREDIENTS

Serves 6

2 pounds rhubarb, cut in
 2-inch lengths
6 tablespoons sugar
finely grated zest and juice of
 2 oranges
1 cup unbleached all-purpose flour
½ cup vegan margarine, chilled
 and cubed
6 tablespoons brown sugar
1¼ cups ground almonds

1 Preheat the oven to 350°F. Place the rhubarb in a shallow oven-proof dish.

2 Sprinkle the sugar onto the rhubarb and add the grated orange zest and orange juice.

3 Sift the flour into a mixing bowl and add the margarine. Rub the margarine into the flour until the mixture resembles bread crumbs.

4 Add the brown sugar and ground almonds and mix well.

NUTRITION NOTES	
Per portion:	
Calories	441
Protein	7.4g
Fat	26.8g
Saturated Fat	6.20g
Carbohydrate	45.4g
Fiber	4.1g
Iron	1.7mg
Calcium	223mg

5 Spoon the crumble mixture onto the fruit. Bake for 40 minutes, until the top is browned and the fruit is cooked. Serve warm.

BREADS AND BAKED GOODS

Homemade breads are simply unbeatable. The taste of the bread and the wonderful aroma that fills your kitchen as it bakes will amply justify the time spent making it. What is more, using whole-wheat and unbleached flour will ensure that your bread is nutritious, unlike the many vitamin-depleted bread products available commercially. Vegan baked goods and cookies—including savory scones, cookies, muffins and cakes—make the most of soy products and whole-food flavorings.

Focaccia

This is a flattish bread, originating from Genoa in Italy, made with flour, olive oil and salt. There are many regional variations, including stuffed varieties, and versions topped with onions, olives or herbs.

Ingredients

Makes 1 loaf
1 ounce fresh yeast
3½ cups unbleached all-purpose flour
2 teaspoons salt
5 tablespoons olive oil
2 teaspoons coarse sea salt

1 Dissolve the yeast in ½ cup warm water. Let stand for 10 minutes. Sift the flour into a large bowl, make a well in the center, and add the yeast, salt and 2 tablespoons oil. Mix in the flour and add more water to make a dough.

2 Turn out onto a floured surface and knead the dough for about 10 minutes, until smooth and elastic. Return to the bowl, cover with a cloth, and let rise in a warm place for 2–2½ hours, until the dough has doubled in size.

3 Punch down the dough and knead again for a few minutes. Press into an oiled 10-inch tart pan, and cover with a damp cloth. Let to rise for 30 minutes.

4 Preheat the oven to 400°F. Poke the dough all over with your fingers, to make little dimples in the surface. Pour the remaining oil over the dough, using a pastry brush to take it to the edges. Sprinkle with the salt.

5 Bake for 20–25 minutes, until the bread is a pale golden color. Carefully remove from the pan and let cool on a rack. The bread is best eaten on the same day, but it also freezes very well.

Nutrition Notes	
Per loaf:	
Calories	1858
Protein	46.0g
Fat	60.5g
Saturated Fat	8.66g
Carbohydrate	301.2g
Fiber	12.4g
Iron	8.6mg
Calcium	560mg

Olive Bread

Olive breads are popular all over the Mediterranean. For this Greek recipe use rich oily olives or those marinated in herbs rather than the canned ones.

INGREDIENTS

Makes 2 loaves
2 red onions, thinly sliced
2 tablespoons olive oil
1⅓ cups pitted black or green olives
7 cups unbleached all-purpose flour
1½ teaspoons salt
4 teaspoons active dry yeast
3 tablespoons each roughly chopped
    parsley, cilantro or mint

1 Fry the onions in the oil until soft. Roughly chop the olives.

2 Put the flour, salt, yeast and parsley, cilantro or mint in a large bowl with the olives and fried onions and pour in 2 cups luke warm water.

3 Mix into a dough using a round-bladed knife, adding a little more water if the mixture feels dry.

4 Turn out onto a lightly floured surface and knead for about 10 minutes. Put in a clean bowl, cover with plastic wrap and set aside in a warm place until doubled in size.

5 Preheat the oven to 425°F. Lightly grease two baking sheets. Turn the dough onto a floured surface and cut in half. Shape into two rounds and place on the baking sheets. Cover loosely with lightly oiled plastic wrap and set aside until doubled in size.

NUTRITION NOTES	
Per loaf:	
Calories	1515
Protein	44.8g
Fat	21.7g
Saturated Fat	4.3g
Carbohydrate	287g
Fiber	15.7g
Iron	9.2mg
Calcium	608mg

6 Slash the tops of the loaves with a knife, then bake for 40 minutes or until the loaves sound hollow when tapped on the bottom. Transfer to a wire rack to cool.

Polenta and Bell Pepper Bread

Full of Mediterranean flavor, this satisfying, sunshine-colored bread is best eaten while still warm, drizzled with olive oil.

INGREDIENTS

Makes 2 loaves

1½ cups polenta
1 teaspoon salt
3 cups unbleached all-purpose flour, plus extra for dusting
1 teaspoon baking soda
1 teaspoon sugar
¼-ounce envelope active dry yeast
1 red bell pepper, roasted, peeled and diced
1 tablespoon olive oil

1 Combine the polenta, salt, flour, baking soda, sugar and yeast in a large bowl. Stir in the diced red pepper, then make a well in the center of the mixture.

2 Add 1¼ cups warm water and the oil, then mix into a soft dough. Knead the dough on a lightly floured surface for 10 minutes, until smooth and elastic. Place in an oiled bowl, cover with oiled plastic wrap and let rise in a warm place until the dough has doubled in size.

3 Punch down the dough, knead lightly, then divide in two. Shape each piece into an oblong and place in the pans. Cover with oiled plastic wrap and let rise for 45 minutes. Preheat the oven to 425°F.

4 Bake the bread for 30 minutes, until golden—the loaves should sound hollow when they are tapped underneath. Let sit on the baking sheet for 5 minutes, then turn out onto a wire rack to cool.

NUTRITION NOTES	
Per loaf:	
Calories	1011
Protein	30.6g
Fat	13.2g
Saturated Fat	1.91g
Carbohydrate	205.2g
Fiber	8.6g
Iron	5.8mg
Calcium	260mg

Whole-wheat Sunflower Bread

Sunflower seeds give a nutty crunchiness to this hearty whole-wheat loaf. Serve with a chunk of vegan cheese and rich tomato chutney.

INGREDIENTS

Makes 1 loaf
4 cups whole-wheat flour
½ teaspoon active dry yeast
½ teaspoon salt
½ cup sunflower seeds,
    plus extra for sprinkling

1 Grease and lightly flour a 1-pound loaf pan. Combine the flour, yeast, salt and sunflower seeds in a large bowl. Make a well in the center and gradually stir in 1¼ cups warm water. Mix vigorously with a wooden spoon to form a soft, sticky dough. The dough should be quite wet and sticky, so don't be tempted to add any extra flour.

NUTRITION NOTES

Per loaf:

Calories	1748
Protein	69.9g
Fat	38.4g
Saturated Fat	4.24g
Carbohydrate	298.8g
Fiber	44.1g
Iron	21.9mg
Calcium	239mg

2 Cover the bowl with a damp dish towel and let the dough rise in a warm place for 45–50 minutes or until doubled in size.

3 Preheat the oven to 400°F. Turn out the dough onto a lightly floured work surface and knead for 10 minutes, until elastic—the dough will still be quite sticky, but resist the temptation to add more flour.

4 Form the dough into a rectangle and place in the loaf pan. Sprinkle the top with sunflower seeds. Cover with a damp dish towel and let rise again for another 15 minutes.

5 Bake for 40–45 minutes, until golden. When ready, the loaf should sound hollow when tapped underneath. Let sit for 5 minutes, then turn out of the pan and cool on a wire rack.

Banana and Cardamom Bread

The combination of banana and cardamom is delicious in this soft-textured moist bread. It is perfect for a snack, served with vegan margarine and fruit jam.

INGREDIENTS

Makes 1 loaf
⅔ cup warm water
1 teaspoon active dry yeast
pinch of sugar
10 cardamom pods
3½ cups unbleached all-purpose flour
1 teaspoon salt
2 tablespoons malt extract
2 ripe bananas, mashed
1 teaspoon sesame seeds

1 Put the water in a small bowl. Sprinkle the yeast on top, add the sugar and mix well. Let stand for 10 minutes.

2 Split the cardamom pods. Remove the seeds and chop them finely.

3 Sift the flour and salt into a mixing bowl and make a well in the center. Add the yeast mixture with the malt extract, chopped cardamom seeds and bananas.

4 Gradually incorporate the flour and mix to form a soft dough, adding a little extra water if necessary. Turn the dough onto a lightly floured surface and knead for 5 minutes, until smooth and elastic. Return to the clean bowl, cover with a damp dish towel and let rise for 2 hours, until the dough has doubled in size.

NUTRITION NOTES	
Per loaf:	
Calories	1536
Protein	48.0g
Fat	6.0g
Saturated Fat	1.2g
Carbohydrate	342.6g
Fiber	13.8g
Iron	7.8mg
Calcium	570mg

5 Preheat the oven to 425°F. Grease a baking sheet. Turn the dough onto a lightly floured surface, knead briefly, then shape into a braid. Place the braid on a plastic sheet and cover loosely with a plastic bag, ballooning it to trap the air. Let sit until well risen.

6 Brush the braid lightly with water and sprinkle with the sesame seeds. Bake for 10 minutes, then lower the oven temperature to 400°F. Cook for 15 more minutes or until the loaf sounds hollow when tapped underneath. Cool on a wire rack.

COOK'S TIP

Make sure the bananas are really ripe before using, so that they impart maximum flavor to the bread.

If you prefer, place the dough in one piece in a 1-pound loaf pan and bake for an extra 5 minutes.

Chive and Potato Scones

These little scones should be fairly thin with soft insides and crisp outsides. Serve them for breakfast.

Ingredients

Makes 20
1 pound potatoes
1 cup unbleached all-purpose
  flour, sifted
2 tablespoons olive oil
2 tablespoons snipped chives
oil, for greasing
salt and freshly ground black pepper
vegan spread, for topping (optional)

1 Cook the potatoes in a saucepan of boiling, salted water for about 20 minutes, until tender, then drain thoroughly. Return the potatoes to the clean pan and mash them. Preheat a griddle or frying pan.

2 Add the flour, olive oil and snipped chives with a little salt and pepper to the hot mashed potato in the pan. Mix into a soft dough.

—— Cook's Tip ——

Cook the scones over low heat so that the outsides do not burn before the insides are cooked through.

3 Roll out the dough on a well-floured surface to a thickness of ¼-inch and stamp out rounds with a 2-inch round cookie cutter. Lightly grease the griddle or frying pan with oil.

4 Cook the scones, in batches, on the hot griddle or frying pan for 10 minutes, turning once, until they are golden on both sides. Keep the heat low. Serve warm, with a little vegan spread, if desired.

—— Nutrition Notes ——

Per scone:

Calories	45
Protein	0.9g
Fat	1.2g
Saturated Fat	0.1g
Carbohydrate	8.0g
Fiber	0.4g
Iron	0.2mg
Calcium	9.4mg

Orange Shortbread Fingers

INGREDIENTS

Makes 18
½ cup vegan margarine
¼ cup sugar, plus extra for dusting
finely grated zest of 2 oranges
1½ cups unbleached all-purpose flour

NUTRITION NOTES	
Per shortbread:	
Calories	91
Protein	0.9g
Fat	5.3g
Saturated Fat	1.6g
Carbohydrate	10.5g
Fiber	0.3g
Iron	0.2mg
Calcium	14.6mg

1 Preheat the oven to 375°F. Beat the margarine and sugar together until they are soft and creamy. Beat in the orange zest.

2 Gradually add the flour and gently pull the dough together to form a soft ball. Roll the dough out on a lightly floured surface until about ½-inch thick. Cut it into fingers, sprinkle on a little extra sugar, prick with a fork and bake for about 20 minutes or until the shortbread fingers are a light golden color.

Double Chocolate Chip Muffins

Everyone loves chocolate, and these rich moist muffins have a double dose. They are best when still warm and the chunks of chocolate are melted and gooey.

INGREDIENTS

Makes 8
2 ounces coconut milk
1¼ cups boiling water
2 cups self-rising flour
1 tablespoon baking powder
pinch of salt
generous ¼ cup unsweetened
   cocoa powder
¼ cup light brown sugar
¼ cup sunflower oil
6 ounces vegan dark chocolate

--- NUTRITION NOTES ---

Per muffin:

Calories	369
Protein	5.0g
Fat	17.3g
Saturated Fat	8.61g
Carbohydrate	51.4g
Fiber	2.9g
Iron	2.1mg
Calcium	147mg

--- COOK'S TIP ---

Only cook with good quality bittersweet chocolate that has a minimum content of 50 percent cocoa solids.

1 Preheat the oven to 350°F. Combine the boiling water and the coconut milk in a bowl. Stir until dissolved, then set aside until cool. Break up the chocolate into chunks.

2 Sift together the flour and baking powder, and add the salt and cocoa powder. Stir in the sugar.

3 Make a well in the center and pour in the coconut milk and oil. Mix well. Stir in the chocolate.

4 Spoon the mixture into eight paper muffin cases set in a muffin pan and bake for 15 minutes. Transfer the muffins to a wire rack to cool.

Date and Orange Oat Cookies

The fragrant aroma of orange permeates the kitchen when these cookies are baking. Orange is a classic partner with dates and both add a richness to the crumbly oat cookies.

INGREDIENTS

Makes 25
¾ cup dark brown sugar
10 tablespoons vegan margarine
Finely grated zest of 1 unwaxed orange
1¼ cups self-rising whole-wheat
    flour, sifted
1 teaspoon baking powder
⅔ cup medium oatmeal
½ cup dried dates, roughly chopped

1 Preheat the oven to 350°F. Line two baking sheets with greaseproof paper. Place the sugar and margarine in a bowl and beat together until light and fluffy. Mix in the orange zest.

2 Fold in the flour, baking powder and oatmeal. Add the dates and mix until combined.

3 Place heaping tablespoonfuls of the mixture onto the baking sheets, spacing them well apart to let the mixture spread. Bake for 15-20 minutes, until golden.

4 Let cool slightly, then transfer the cookies to wire racks to cool completely.

VARIATIONS

Replace the dates with dried chopped apricots, raisins or figs.

NUTRITION NOTES

Per cookie:

Calories	106
Protein	1.3g
Fat	5.3g
Saturated Fat	1.75g
Carbohydrate	14.3g
Fiber	0.9g
Iron	0.5mg
Calcium	12mg

Pineapple and Ginger Upside-Down Cake

A light and moist cake that has a sticky ginger glaze. It is superb as a dessert served with homemade dairy-free custard or thick soy cream.

Ingredients

Serves 8

1½ tablespoons vegan margarine
2 pieces crystallized ginger, chopped, plus ¼ cup syrup
1 pound can pineapple chunks in natural juice, drained
2¼ cups whole-wheat self-rising flour
1 tablespoon baking powder
1 teaspoon ground ginger
1 teaspoon ground cinnamon
½ cups light brown sugar
1 cup soy milk
3 tablespoons sunflower oil
1 banana

────── Nutrition Notes ──────	
Per portion:	
Calories	279
Protein	5.3g
Fat	7.5g
Saturated Fat	1.44g
Carbohydrate	50.7g
Fiber	3.1g
Iron	2.4mg
Calcium	59mg

1 Preheat the oven to 350°F. Grease and line an 8-inch cake pan. Melt the margarine in a small pan, and stir in the ginger syrup, and heat over high heat until thickened. Pour the mixture into the prepared cake pan and level the surface.

2 Arrange the crystallized ginger and one-third of the pineapple pieces in the bottom of the pan.

3 Sift together the flour, baking powder and spices into a bowl. Mix in the sugar.

4 Blend together the milk, oil, the remaining pineapple and banana in a food processor or blender until almost smooth, then add the mixture to the flour. Mix until thoroughly combined. Spoon the mixture over the pineapple and ginger pieces in the pan.

5 Bake for 45 minutes, until a skewer inserted into the center of the cake comes out clean. Let cool slightly, then place a serving plate over the pan and turn upside down. Serve hot or cold, with homemade custard or soy cream.

Parsnip Cake with Creamy Orange Icing

INGREDIENTS

Serves 10
2¼ cups whole-wheat self-rising flour
1 tablespoon baking powder
1 teaspoon ground cinnamon
1 teaspoon freshly ground nutmeg
7 tablespoons vegan margarine
scant ½ cup light brown sugar
9 ounces parsnips, coarsely grated
1 medium banana, mashed
finely grated zest and juice of
   1 unwaxed orange

For the topping
8-ounce container vegan cream cheese
3 tablespoons confectioners' sugar
juice of 1 small orange
fine strips of orange peel

1 Preheat the oven to 350°F. Lightly grease and line the bottom of a 2-pound loaf pan.

2 Sift the flour, baking powder and spices into a large bowl. Add any bran remaining in the sieve.

3 Melt the margarine in a pan, add the sugar and stir until dissolved. Make a well in the flour mixture, then add the melted margarine and sugar. Mix in the parsnips, banana and orange zest and juice. Spoon the mixture into the prepared pan and level the top with the back of a spoon.

4 Bake for 45–50 minutes, until a skewer inserted into the center of the cake comes out clean. Let cool before removing from the pan.

5 For the topping, beat together the cream cheese, confectioners' sugar, orange juice and strips of orange peel, until smooth. Spread the topping evenly over the cake.

NUTRITION NOTES	
Per portion:	
Calories	257
Protein	4.0g
Fat	11.7g
Saturated Fat	3.72g
Carbohydrate	36.2g
Fiber	3.5g
Iron	1.6mg
Calcium	54mg

INFORMATION FILE

USEFUL ADDRESSES

ORGANIZATIONS
American Vegan Society
P.O. Box H
Malaga, NJ 08328
Tel: (609) 694-2887

EarthSave International
444 NE Ravenna Boulevard
Suite 205
Seattle, WA 09105
www.earthsave.org

The EnviroLink Network
5805 Forbes Avenue, 2nd Floor
Pittsburgh, PA 15217
Tel: (412) 420-6400
www.envirolink.org

FARM (Farm Animal Reform Movement)
P.O. Box 30654
Bethesda, MD 20824
Tel: (301) 530-1737
www.farmusa.org

NAVS (North American Vegetarian Society)
P.O. Box 72
Dolgeville, NY 13329
Tel: (518) 568-7970
www.cyberveg.org/navs

PETA (People for the Ethical Treatment of Animals)
501 Front Street
Norfolk, VA 23510
Tel: (757) 622-PETA
www.peta.com

Vegan Action
P.O. Box 4353
Berkeley, CA 94704
Tel: (510) 548-7377
www.vegan.org

Vegan Outreach
211 Indian Dive
Pittsburgh, PA 15238
Tel: (412) 968-0268
www.veganoutreach.org

Vegetarian Resource Center
P.O. Box 38-1068
Cambridge, MA 02238
Tel: (617) 625-3790

Vegetarian Union of North America
P.O. Box 9710
Washington, D.C. 20016
www.ivu.org/vuna

MARKETS
Rella Good Cheese Company
P.O. Box 5020
Santa Rosa, CA 95402
Tel: (707) 572-7050
www.rella.com

Apple Valley Market
9067 U.S. 31
Berrien Springs, MI 49103
Tel: (800) BERRIEN

Eden Foods, Inc.
701 Tecumseh Road
Clinton, MI 49236
Tel: (517) 456-7424
www.eden-foods.com

Harvest Direct
P.O. Box 4514
Decateur, IL 62525
Tel: (800) 8-FLAVOR

Heartland Bread Company
620 Coleman Boulevard
Mt. Pleasant, SC 29464
Tel: (803) 849-9675

Whole Foods Market
601 North Lamar
Austin, TX 78703
www.wholefoods.com

CANADA
Canadian Vegans for Animal Rights
c/o General Delivery
Port Berry
Ontario LOB 1NO
Tel: (416) 985 3308

Canada EarthSave Society
Suite 103–1093 West Broadway
Vancouver
BC V6H 1E2
Tel: (604) 731 5885

SELECTED BIBLIOGRAPHY

Animal Factories, Jim Mason and Peter Singer (Crown, New York, 1980)

Animal Liberation: A Graphic Guide, Lori Gruen, Peter Singer and David Hine (Camden Press, 1987)

Animal Rights and Human Obligations, Tom Regan and Peter Singer (Prentice Hall, New Jersey, 1976)

Animals, Politics and Morality, Robert Garner (MUP, 1993)

The Civilised Alternative, Jon Wynne-Tyson (Centaur Press, 1986)

Food Fit for Humans, Frank Wilson (Daniel, 1975)

Food for a Future, Jon Wynne-Tyson (Centaur Press, 1979)

In Defence of Living Things, Christine Townend (Wentworth, Sydney, 1980)

The Moral Status of Animals, Stephen R.L.Clark (OUP, 1977)

The Philosophy of Compassion, Esmé Wynne-Tyson (Centaur Press, 1970)

Vegan Nutrition, Gill Langley (The Vegan Society, 1995)

Why Vegan, Kath Clements (GMP, 1995)

INDEX